HOLY HEROES

THE GOSPEL ACCORDING
TO DC & MARVEL

SCOTT BAYLES

FOREWORD BY H. MICHAEL BREWER

JUDSON PRESS
PUBLISHERS SINCE 1824

Join our mailing list for updates and special offers.
www.judsonpress.com/mailing_list.cfm

HOLY HEROES: THE GOSPEL ACCORDING TO DC & MARVEL
© 2016 by Judson Press, Valley Forge, PA 19482-0851
All rights reserved.

Judson Press has made every effort to trace the ownership of all quotes. In the event of a question arising from the use of a quote, we regret any error made and will be pleased to make the necessary correction in future printings and editions of this book.

The Holy Bible, English Standard Version® (ESV®), copyright © 2001 by Crossway, a publishing ministry of Good News Publishers. Used by permission. All rights reserved.

God's Word Translation (GW), copyright © 1995 by God's Word to the Nations. Used by permission of Baker Publishing Group.

Good News Bible, the Bible in Today's English Version. Copyright © American Bible Society, 1976. Used by permission.

The Holy Bible, King James Version.

The Holman Christian Standard Bible®, Copyright © 1999, 2000, 2002, 2003, 2009 by Holman Bible Publishers. Used by permission. Holman Christian Standard Bible®, Holman CSB®, and HCSB® are federally registered trademarks of Holman Bible Publishers.

The Living Bible, copyright © 1971. Used by permission of Tyndale House Publishers, Inc., Wheaton, IL 60189. All right reserved.

THE MESSAGE. Copyright © by Eugene H. Peterson 1993, 1994, 1995, 1996, 2000, 2001, 2002. Used by permission of NavPress Publishing Group.

The New American Standard Bible, © 1960, 1962, 1963, 1968, 1971, 1972, 1973, 1975, 1977, 1995 by The Lockman Foundation. Used by permission.

The Holy Bible, New Century Version, copyright © 1987, 1988, 1991 by Word Publishing, Nashville, TN 37214. Used by permission.

The HOLY BIBLE, NEW INTERNATIONAL VERSION®. NIV®. Copyright © 1973, 1978, 1984, 2011 by Biblica, Inc.™ Used by permission. All rights reserved worldwide.

The New King James Version. Copyright © 1972, 1984 by Thomas Nelson Inc.

The *Holy Bible*. New Living Translation copyright © 1996, 2004, 2007 by Tyndale House Foundation. Used by permission of Tyndale House Publishers, Inc. Carol Stream, Illinois 60188. All rights reserved.

Interior design and cover design by Wendy Ronga and Hampton Design Group.

Library of Congress Cataloging-in-Publication Data
Cataloging-in-Publication Data available upon request. Contact cip@judsonpress.com.

Printed in the U.S.A.
First printing, 2016.

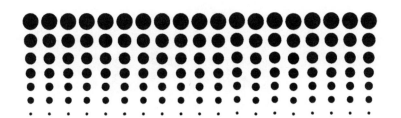

FOR MY SON, YESHUA.

YOU'RE THE ROBIN
TO MY BATMAN,

THE BUCKY TO MY CAP'.

ANY HERO WOULD BE PROUD TO
HAVE YOU AS A SIDEKICK.

CONTENTS

FOREWORD

If you've bought this book, congratulations on a wise choice. Feel free to skip the next couple of pages and go straight to the good stuff.

If you're leafing through this book and wondering if it's worth your time and money, let me reassure you. I've been a pastor nearly four decades and a superhero fan even longer. I have a shelf filled with well-worn Bibles in sundry translations and a room filled with comics. A few years back I even wrote a book about the spiritual message embedded in the sprawling superhero saga. I've spent most of my life hanging out at that odd intersection of Faith and Comic Books, so you can trust me when I tell you that Scott Bayles is the real deal.

From comic books to fan conventions, from classic television shows to recent blockbuster movies, Scott embraces the whole superhero scene. His breadth of knowledge earns him a gold star in the grade book of fandom. My fellow pastor knows his Bible, too, and he grounds this book in solid Christian teaching.

I love the author's clever approach to comic book icons, often bringing out a nuance that I never thought of before. Many of these characters have a long history, and Scott has a knack for locating overlooked nuggets. Superman's girlfriend as an icon of truth? Black Widow as the exemplar of new beginnings? Who'd have thunk it?

I appreciate the broad scope of the book. Of course, comic book giants like Superman, Batman, and Spider-Man get time in the limelight. You'll find most of the popular heroes in here. But we are also treated to supporting characters such as Lois Lane and the more-or-less villainous Star Sapphire. (I'm disappointed that Matter-Eater Lad didn't make the cut, but this is a delightful mix nonetheless.)

I'm also grateful that Scott doesn't wander far from the Bible. Familiar passages and stories from the old Book take on fresh applications and new insights when laid alongside these stories of fantasy heroes. Some comparisons are obvious, such as Iron Man and the gospel armor of Ephesians. But others scintillate with originality—for example, Thor and the prodigal son parable. I predict you will find many *Aha!* moments in these pages.

Scott's writing itself is easy-going and companionable, which makes reading *Holy Heroes* like having a conversation with a friend. He's good at summing up decades of backstory in a paragraph or two. And he loves alliteration, those bold-print headings that all start with the same letter.

Most of all in this book, I've enjoyed getting an inside glimpse into the world of cosplay, the pastime of dressing as fantasy, science-fiction, and comic book characters. Except for a couple of years in my childhood when I wore a yellow tablecloth knotted around my neck, I have never dipped a toe into cosplay. (Okay, in the spirit of full disclosure, I'm wearing Batman socks as I write these words, but I don't think that counts.) I'm fascinated by Scott's account of elaborate homemade costumes, donned by himself, his family, his friends, and even members of his church. That Scott can use these costumes as a way to bring hope, encouragement, and good news to others is a tribute both to his sewing abilities and to the infinite creativity of our Maker.

Even if you have zero interest in wearing a domino mask or a utility belt, the adventures of Scott Bayles remind us to offer God whatever know-how, passion, or talent we happen to possess. God does amazing things with unlikely gifts. As you read this book, you will not only get a new perspective on comic book heroes, but you might discover how your particular "super powers" might make a difference in the world.

Perhaps some folks will be put off by Scott's enthusiastic cosplaying. Isn't that a frivolous activity for a follower of Jesus, particularly—ahem!—a minister of the gospel?

I say thee nay!

Oops! I slipped into Thor-speak. Let me try that again.

In fact, cosplay is a thoroughly Christian notion dating all the way back to the apostle Paul. After warning the Roman Christians against destructive lifestyles, the apostle concludes with, "Rather, clothe yourselves with the Lord Jesus Christ..." (Romans 13:14 NIV) Paul's idea, simply put, is that acting like Jesus—spiritually dressing up like Jesus—will gradually make us more like Jesus. As far as we know, Paul never wore a cape or cowl, but I think of him as the father of Christian cosplay because he spent the latter half of his life role-playing Jesus, emulating the teachings and example of his master.

If a superhero outfit inspires someone to try on the virtues of self-sacrifice, courage, and compassion, let the cosplay continue! Both theologians and psychologists agree that we become like those we imitate, and every true hero points toward the Great Hero. At least, that's what Scott Bayles and I believe.

Are you *still* reading this foreword?

'Nuff said already. Jump into the book. Adventure and insight await, and you're in the hands of an excellent tour guide. Follow that guy in the cape. Who knows? He might even have an extra costume for you.

H. Michael Brewer
Author, *Who Needs a Superhero?*
Pastor, Blue Ash Presbyterian Church

ACKNOWLEDGMENTS

I owe a debt of thanks to many heroes who helped this book become a reality.

Editors and staff at Judson Press, thank you for your patience and willingness to take a risk on a novice writer.

Blooming Grove Christian Church, thank you for allowing me to test-run many of these chapters as Sunday morning sermons.

My mother, thank you for buying my first comic book and encouraging me throughout my writing endeavors.

Brian Morris, thanks for your early encouragement and insights as a fellow writer.

Winfield Strock, thanks for all the constructive criticism and for challenging me to become a better author.

Chris Kelly, thanks for your proofreading and enthusiasm about this book.

Zac Pensol, thanks for lending me your time and artistic talents.

My fellow Costumers for Christ (there are too many of you to list), thank you for all the work you do in helping to share Christ through comics and cosplay.

And finally, thanks to my wife and kids for joining me in my geeky adventures.

You are all my heroes.

INTRODUCTION

I'll come out and say this right from the start: I'm a really big geek.

I wear that name like a badge of honor because I've earned it. I started collecting comic books almost as soon as I could read. Wednesdays were my favorite day of the week growing up because Wednesday is new comic book day. Each week I pedaled my bike to the comic book store in the Piggly-Wiggly strip plaza to snag the latest issues. Even before my weekly pilgrimages to the comic book store began, I spent countless Saturday mornings laying belly-down on the carpet of our living room watching *The Super Friends* and other Hanna-Barbera cartoons such as *Space Ghost* and *Birdman*.

Today, my comic book collection numbers in the thousands. And, now that I'm a father of three, I still find myself lying on the floor in our living room watching superhero cartoons such as *Justice League Unlimited*, *Young Justice*, and *Ultimate Spider-Man*.

If you ask me, there's never been a better time to be a comic book geek! For more than a decade now, we've enjoyed watching our favorite comic book characters in big-screen blockbusters such as *The Amazing Spider-Man*, *The Dark Knight Trilogy*, *The Avengers*, *Guardians of the Galaxy*, and *Man of Steel*. Add to that the increasing number of superhero TV series, including CW's *Arrow* and *The Flash*, Netflix's *Daredevil*, CBS's *Supergirl*, and ABC's *Agents of S.H.I.E.L.D.*, to name just a few. However, live-action superheroes aren't confined to movie theaters and television screens. Superhero costuming, or *cosplay*, has exploded into pop culture in the past few years. It's a fundamental part of comic book conventions, and image-hosting websites such as Imgur and

Tumblr are rife with pictures of enthusiastic fans clad in elaborate costumes, capes, and cowls.

Six years ago, I took my geekiness to the next level. My family and I lived in a small mining town in southern Illinois just a few short miles from the real-life city of Metropolis (not at all the basis for Superman's hometown, incidentally). Back in 1972, city representatives adopted Superman as their official mascot. Since 1978 the city has hosted an annual celebration of Superman each summer. Think county fair meets comic book convention. To commemorate the 30th Annual Superman Celebration, the city set their sights on a Guinness World Record for the largest gathering of people dressed as Superman. I was intrigued…but hesitant.

I had never even heard the word *cosplay*, and the last time I wore a superhero costume I was five years old. It was one of those vinyl Halloween costumes that fit more like a baptismal gown and even had Batman's name emblazoned across the chest in case people couldn't tell who I was supposed to be. Do you remember the cheap rubber band on the back of those plastic masks? It lasted all of ten seconds before it snapped, and I toted the mask from house to house the rest of the night. Maybe having the name plastered across the chest wasn't such a bad idea after all.

Despite my misgivings, I leapt at the chance for my then two-year-old son and me to get our names in the Guinness World Record Book! I had a little sewing experience growing up, so I bought some fabric, tore apart a set of thermal underwear to get a pattern, and sewed myself a super-suit. In hindsight, it looked pretty pathetic. The iron-on symbol bled and ran in the ninety-degree heat, and I was in no condition to be wearing spandex! But I wasn't alone. One hundred nineteen other super-fans descended upon the city in their own Superman costumes. Some were store-bought, some were even worse than mine, but others flawlessly reproduced the iconic costumes worn by Christopher Reeve or Dean Cain. All of us huddled together in the shadow of the 15-foot bronze Superman statue standing proudly in the center of town. Thus, our names were immortalized as participants 54 and 55 in the 2008 Guinness World Record Book.

In spite of the sweat stains and lack of sinew beneath the spandex, I think that my son and I were kind of cute in our matching costumes, and I even received a couple of compliments from other costume-clad Superman fans. Anticipating another Superman Celebration the next year and with Halloween only a few months away, I determined to make new and improved costumes for the whole family. I did. And I didn't stop there. Six years and countless costumes later, we decided that our enthusiasm for superheroes and our love for the Lord needn't be relegated to two separate spheres; rather, we could use our comic and costuming hobbies as a means of sharing the love of God and the message of Jesus with our fellow geeks.

Along with a few of our costuming companions, my wife, Ashley, and I started a ministry that we call Costumers for Christ. Our inaugural event took us back to Metropolis, where our team of superhero impersonators handed out free bottles of water to super-fans in the sweltering summer heat. The bottles featured our Costumers for Christ logo and a quote from Jesus speaking to the woman at the well: "Anyone who drinks this water will soon become thirsty again. But those who drink the water I give will never be thirsty again. It becomes a fresh, bubbling spring within them, giving them eternal life" (John 4:13-14, NLT). In three hours we gave away twenty cases of water and posed for innumerable pictures with comic book fans!

Since then Costumers for Christ has visited cancer patients at a major children's hospital, participated in fundraisers for local charities, read to excited children at elementary schools, and attended comic book conventions all over the Midwest, where we've given away hundreds of copies of *The Amazing Gospel*—a comic book adaptation of the life of Jesus.[1] And we do it all while dressed as our favorite superheroes!

This ministry has convinced me that comic book heroes can teach valuable spiritual lessons. In fact, I liken superhero stories to modern-day parables similar to those used by Jesus to illustrate the spiritual principles that he preached. The Bible says, "Jesus used many similar stories and illustrations to teach the people as much as they could understand. In fact, in his public ministry he never taught without using parables" (Mark 4:33-34, NLT). Jesus knew that people would connect with his teaching if he presented it in the form of a relevant, relatable story. That's what I hope this book will do for you. I believe that the stories of comic book heroes such as Batman, Spider-Man, and Wonder Woman can help superhero fans connect with the timeless truths of God's Word. So if you're a fan of comic books and a follower of Christ—or if you'd just like to know more about one or the other—this book is for you! So, read. Enjoy. And, hopefully, you'll discover, as I have, that Jesus is the greatest superhero of them all!

NOTES

1. Daniel Schwabauer (writer) and Gabriel Valles (artist), *The Amazing Gospel* (Crosswind Comics, 2007).

1
SUPERMAN

Superman has always been my favorite comic book hero. Like so many other kids who grew up with Superman, I often pulled a towel out of the linen closet, threw it over my shoulders, and flew around the living room. I was just three years old when my mom replaced my towel with an honest-to-goodness Superman cape from Sears. When I tied that little red cape around my neck, I was convinced I could fly. I would climb up on our dining room table, build up as much speed as I could, and take a flying leap into the kitchen. Amazingly, I never hit the ground! My mom zipped through the house and snatched me out of the air before I splattered myself across the linoleum. I still have that little red cape from Sears. I've tenderly cared for it and handed it down to my son and daughters. Watching them swoop and swoosh through the house always brings a smile to my face.

Since the debut of my first homemade Superman costume in Metropolis, I've sewn more capes and costumes than I can count. Every year I find at least one or two reasons to cosplay as the Man of Steel. Three years ago, for instance, our local elementary school hosted a book fair with the theme "Reading Saves the Day!" They invited real-life heroes from the community, including a firefighter, police officer, and an EMT. They also invited my wife and me to appear as Supergirl and Superman. Seated in the school gymnasium, we read *Superhero ABC* to a crowded circle of second graders.[1] Just last month I donned my Superman cape yet again when Costumers for Christ partnered with our local WalMart to raise money for Children's Miracle Network. And, since Superman is a perennial favorite, I'm sure that I'll find many more excuses to cosplay as the big blue Boy Scout for years to come.

Superman has been saving the day since 1939, when he first graced the pages of Action Comics. Prior to Superman bursting onto the scene, the concept of spandex-wearing superheroes didn't exist. He initiated the superhero genre and remains a fan-favorite to this day. Over the years, he has appeared in comic books, radio programs, cartoons, multiple television series, and a half-dozen feature films.

During that time, fans, commentators, and movie reviewers have identified striking similarities between Superman and Jesus. The Man of Steel is a literary Christ-figure—that is, a fictional character made in the image of Jesus. Thus, the story of Superman reflects the gospel story in multiple ways. It's the story of a father in the heavens who sends his only son to earth "with powers and abilities far beyond those of mortal men," to be raised in a small town by adoptive parents, and ultimately save the world. But it's not enough to simply identify these similarities without also asking what we can learn from them. Can Superman really help us to better understand Jesus and draw closer to him? To help answer that question, I'd like to zero in on three of the plentiful parallels between Superman and our Savior. The first is Superman's secret identity, or his split persona, as I call it.

SPLIT PERSONAS

When Jerry Siegel and Joe Shuster created the world's first superhero, they knew that he couldn't be running around in tights and a cape twenty-four hours a day. A superhero needs an ordinary life too, something to which readers can relate. Thus, the secret identity of Clark Kent, mild-mannered reporter, was born. But beneath the glasses and fedora hides his alter ego—Superman, who fights a "never-ending battle" for "truth, justice, and the American way."

For those unfamiliar with the tale, just moments before the distant planet Krypton explodes, a scientist and visionary named Jor-El places his infant son in a rocket ship bound for Earth. It crash lands on the property of modest farmers, Jonathan and Martha Kent, who raise the boy as their own in the rural Kansas town of Smallville.

In the 2013 Superman movie, *Man of Steel*, Jor-El appears to his now-adult son in the form of a hologram and assures him, "You are as much a child of Earth now as you are of Krypton…. You had the best of both and were meant to be the bridge between two worlds." As Clark Kent, he can experience humanity firsthand. As Superman, he can be humanity's greatest hero. Of course, Superman's split persona reminds us that our Savior—the one true Superhero—also has a dual nature.

The Bible tells us that Jesus is both fully human and fully God. In the Gospel of John, for instance, we learn, "Before anything else existed, there was Christ, with God. He has always been alive and is himself God. He created everything there is—nothing exists that he didn't make…. And Christ became a human being and lived on earth among us" (John 1:1,14, TLB). Jesus, the Word of God made flesh, is the answer to Solomon's centuries-old question: "Will God really live on earth among people?" (2 Chronicles 6:18, NLT).

According to the Bible, the God who spoke the universe into existence stepped down from heaven and entered our world. The arms of a teenage virgin cradled him. Angels watched with wonder as the creator of the cosmos took his first steps. Jesus may have been pushed around by the neighborhood bully. He probably scraped his knees on the cobbled streets of Nazareth. One thing is for sure: Jesus was completely divine, yet completely human at the same time—fully God and fully human.

Of course, Superman's split persona prevents people from seeing Clark Kent for who he really is. In *Superman/Batman* #9, Clark attempts to explain the importance of his secret identity to his teenage cousin, Kara Zor-El (soon to be Supergirl). "Still," she doubts, "nobody recognizes you just because you wear a pair of glasses?"

Moments later, as the two stroll through Metropolis's Centennial Park, Kara is left open-mouthed by an imposing effigy—a 25-foot bronze sculpture of Superman standing in the center of the park with an outstretched arm upon which a bald eagle perches. "Oh my!" she gasps. "This is how they see you? You're their champion. Bigger than life. No wonder the eyeglasses work—nobody would look for *you* dressed like *them*!"[2]

I think that the same is true of God in Christ. Many people fail to recognize Jesus as divine because he looks so human. To paraphrase Supergirl, "Nobody would look for *God* dressed like a *man*!" But that's precisely who Jesus is—God cloaked in humanity.

And isn't that the kind of hero we need? A merely human Jesus could love us and sympathize with our plight, but never save us. A merely divine Jesus would be so far above and beyond us that we could never relate to him or approach him. God knew that we needed a savior who lived among us, but who also had powers and abilities far beyond us. As the God-Man, Jesus is everything we need in a hero.

SUPERPOWERS

In addition to his split persona, Superman also mimics Jesus with his superpowers! Superman has a vast array of superpowers: flight, super-vision, super-speed, super-hearing, even super-breath. But one of the most remarkable of Superman's powers and abilities is his super-strength. The old radio serial of the 1940s boasted that Superman "could change the course of mighty rivers" and "bend steel in his bare hands."

SUPERMAN

One of my favorite scenes from the 1978 film *Superman*, starring Christopher Reeve, demonstrates an array of Superman's powers, including his flight, speed, and strength. It begins with trouble atop the *Daily Planet* building and ends with Superman making his first heroic rescue. Lois Lane hurriedly boards a helicopter scheduled to fly her to an interview with the president when a freak accident sends the helicopter careening off the helipad. Just then, Clark Kent exits the building and spots the damsel in distress. He spins quickly through a revolving door, changing clothes faster than a speeding bullet, and emerges as Superman. Streaking through the air in the nick of time, Superman catches the intrepid reporter in freefall and then gracefully snatches the careening copter, effortlessly lifting it back to the roof, resting it in the center of the helipad. And, of course, the crowd goes wild.[3]

Later in the same film, Superman exhibits further feats of strength as he lands a yacht in the streets of Metropolis, lifts a bus loaded with children to safety, and even raises portions of the California landscape to repair earthquake damage. Of course, Superman's incredible superpowers point us to an even greater power—Jesus.

Jesus isn't just more powerful than a locomotive; he's more powerful than anything we could ever imagine. Jesus possesses the power to turn water into wine, heal diseases, cast out demons, and command the wind and the waves. But that's not all. The Bible says, "Jesus knew that the Father had given him power over everything and that he had come from God and was going back to God" (John 13:3, NCV).

Let me emphasize three of those words from the above Scripture again: *power over everything.*

Jesus possesses power over *everything.*

The fact that Jesus is supremely powerful makes a world of difference to you and me. Think back to the helicopter scene when Superman caught Lois in midair. He calmly reassured her, "Don't worry, miss, I've got you." To which Lois quipped, "You've got me? Who's got you?" When someone as powerful as Superman has you in his arms, what could you possibly worry about? She didn't realize it, but Lois was safe and secure in the arms of her hero. So are you. Jesus once said, "Don't let your hearts be troubled. Trust in God, and trust also in me" (John 14:1, NLT). In other words, "Don't worry, I've got you."

Because Jesus is supremely powerful, there is nothing he can't handle. No situation is too difficult or dangerous. Regardless of the circumstances, Jesus is in control. When a close friend is in the ICU, Jesus is in control. When the economy—national or personal—collapses, Jesus is in control. When tornadoes or terrorists rage out of control, Jesus is still in control. Trust him. You are safe and secure in the arms of Jesus.

In addition to his spilt persona and superpowers, there is one more important way that Superman reflects our Savior: his selfless personality.

SELFLESS PERSONALITIES

One of the things that make Superman so super is his willingness to sacrifice himself for others. No story demonstrates this more clearly than "The Death of Superman."[4] I will never forget a chilly Wednesday afternoon in November of 1992. My dad drove me to the comic book store to buy the newest issue of *Superman*. I never saw anything like it. The line at the comic book store stretched out the door and around the corner as customers waited for hours to get a copy of the issue that sold millions. When I finally made it to the front of the line, the store owner reached beneath the counter and handed me the coveted collector's edition of *Superman* #75.

In the story that resulted in the Man of Steel's murder, a mysterious monster imprisoned far below the surface of the Earth breaks free and wreaks havoc all over the Midwest. This hulking behemoth collapses an interstate overpass, demolishes an eighteen-wheeler in a head-on collision with his fist, and aimlessly destroys whatever catches his eye. A bystander describes him as "the devil incarnate ushering in the end of the world." One of the other heroes, who tries and fails to stop him, dubs the monster "Doomsday."

Superman is the only hero strong enough to face the ferocious beast in a battle that stretches across six issues and several states. Full-page panels decorated each page, stressing the hugeness of the story. As their melee reaches Metropolis, streets are demolished, cars are hurled, and the indestructible fighters crash through buildings. Their final punches send shockwaves, shattering the glass from nearby windows. Bruised and bloody, Superman refuses to give up. Finally, he puts every ounce of strength into one last blow. Like weary boxers, the two contenders collide and then collapse onto the broken pavement.

On the last page, in an image reminiscent of Michelangelo's *Pietà*, Lois whispers to Superman, "You stopped him! You saved us all!" Then the leaf folds out into a three-page splash, as Superman dies in Lois's arms.

I'll be honest with you, I cried when I read that story. Superman was my hero, yet there he lay—broken and lifeless. It shattered my eleven-year-old heart. This story and this image defined for me what it meant to be a hero.

Meanwhile, I was also reading my Bible and listening closely to the stories that I would hear in Sunday school about a hero sent from above to save the world. I made a connection between the two. Superman became the bridge that Jesus walked across.

What Superman did in that comic book, Jesus did in reality. The monster may have been different, but the outcome was the same. The Bible says, "When we were unable to help ourselves, at the moment of our need, Christ died for us, although we were living against God. Very few people will die to save the life of someone else. Although perhaps for a good person someone might possibly die. But God shows his great love for us in this way: Christ died for us while we were still sinners" (Romans 5:6-8, NCV).

Jesus died on the cross to save us from our own sin and to rescue us not just for a time, but for eternity. A couple weeks after *Superman* #75 hit the shelves, I was baptized and entrusted my life to the hero who gave his life for me.

That's why Jesus is my superhero!

He wants to be your hero too.

***

The selfless hero that Superman is in comics and cartoons, Jesus is in reality—and so much more. The story of Superman serves as a modern-day parable pointing us to a God who loves us so much that he gave his only Son to save the world. Could you use a hero right now? Are you in need of Savior to rescue you and keep you safe? No matter what's going on in your life, I want to encourage you to trust in Jesus and embrace him as your own personal Superhero.

NOTES
1. Bob McLeod, *SuperHero ABC* (New York: HarperCollins, 2006).
2. Jeph Loeb (writer) and Ed McGuiness (artist), *Superman/Batman* #9 (DC Comics, 2004).
3. *Superman*, directed by Richard Donner (Warner Bros., 1978).
4. Dan Jurgens (writer and artist), *Superman* #75 (DC Comics, 1992).

2
LOIS LANE

When I was growing up, my family always attended church on Sunday nights. I loved those intimate Sunday evening gatherings. But starting in 1993, I hurried out the door as soon as the closing hymn was sung, rushed home, and plopped down in front of the television to watch the newest episode of *Lois & Clark: The New Adventures of Superman*.

It was a colorful, campy version of Superman that actually focused more on Lois and Clark's budding romance than it did on Superman's heroic exploits. In one episode, titled "Ultra Woman," two twisted sisters plot to destroy the Man of Steel with a beam of red kryptonite. But their scheme backfires when they unwittingly transfer Superman's superhuman abilities to Lois, who then fills in for Clark until they figure out a way to return his powers.[1]

Of course, this wasn't the first time Lois received superpowers, nor would it be the last. The cover of a 1960 issue of *Superman's Girlfriend, Lois Lane* featured Lois in a green and yellow super-suit quipping, "Superman, now that I have super-powers you'll want me for a wife!"[2] More recently, Grant Morrison and Frank Quitely imbued Lois with the Man of Steel's might in their 2005 miniseries, *All-Star Superman*. In this story, Superman creates a serum from his own blood that allows Lois to experience all of his superpowers for twenty-four hours. Superman presents it to Lois for her birthday, and the two enjoy an adventure-filled day that includes a conflict with a time-traveling super-adventurer and a loving embrace on the surface of the moon.[3]

Inspired by the idea of a super-powered couple, I created costumes based on the *All-Star Superman* story for Ashley and me to wear to Metropolis in 2013, which also happened to be our first Costumers for Christ event. Alongside several other costume-clad superheroes, we handed out free bottles of water to sweaty Superman fans in the 90-degree heat and then posed for a seemingly endless stream of pictures in a special photo shoot titled "Superman through the Ages." Ashley's Super-Lois costume finally gave us the opportunity to cosplay as a super-couple and elevated Lois from sidekick to superhero.

The truth is, though, with or without superpowers, Lois Lane is a hero in her own right. During the early days of Superman's career, Lois required rescuing so often that she earned a reputation for being the definitive damsel in distress. Ashley experienced this firsthand when she starred as Lois Lane in a stage play adapted from one of the old 1950s *Superman* television episodes, "The Perils of Superman." A cadre of criminals wearing lead masks employed an old cliché by tying Lois to a set of railroad tracks. Of course, Superman, played by our good friend Keith Howard, leapt to her rescue without a moment to spare.

Over the decades, though, Lois's character evolved into much more than Superman's girlfriend. Even though Lois doesn't ordinarily have superpowers or wear a colorful costume, as a reporter for the *Daily Planet*, she stands shoulder to shoulder with Clark Kent in the fight for truth and justice. Her investigative reporting has helped expose corruption and topple criminal empires. The list of Lois's virtues is long, but her persistent pursuit of truth is perhaps most relevant to spiritual seekers and Christ-followers. Lois's tenacious reporting is fueled by her unquenchable thirst for truth.

An illuminating twist takes place in *Superman: The Man of Steel* #126, where Lois herself gives an interview to a journalism student from her alma mater. After a series of probing questions in a cute little coffee shop on campus, the interview takes a peculiar turn when the eager young reporter asks, "Ms. Lane, if you could be a goddess, what would you be the goddess of?" A bit befuddled, Lois responds, "Heh? Well, that's…hmmm. Interesting question." After a moment of contemplation, Lois finally answers, "How about truth? Objective truth. I'm a journalist, kid! The truth is what I'm all about."[4]

Lois's ambition to be the protector and personification of truth reminds me of another interview that took place within the echoing halls of a Roman palace two millennia ago. Jesus testified before the Roman governor Pontius Pilate, saying, "The reason I was born and came into the world is to testify to the truth. Everyone on the side of truth listens to me" (John 18:37, NIV). The governor responded by inquiring, "What is truth?" (John 18:38).

Pilate's question still reverberates down through history. In a contemporary culture that often denies the existence of objective or absolute truth, the question is more important than ever to answer. What is truth?

Following in Lois's intrepid footsteps, let's investigate this question together.

TRUTH IS REAL

Lois makes a one-page appearance in a Justice League story-arc spanning *JLA* issues #62–64. The Justice League faces a dire threat when Wonder Woman's magical Lasso of Truth breaks in battle. As a result, all of reality begins to unravel. All truth becomes relative, and the Justice League must contend with a world capriciously redefined by the dreams and beliefs of the human race. Instead of objective truth governing the universe, whatever people believe becomes true. In Gotham City, Killer Croc is freed from jail because he says, "It wasn't me." In Ivy Town, scientist Ray Palmer (aka The Atom) racks his brain when two plus one equals four. The moon turns to green cheese, and a flat earth becomes the center of the universe. The Justice League concludes that truth itself has been broken.

In the midst of this madness, Lois pitches a story to her editor-in-chief, Perry White, about a congressman who supposedly murdered his mistress when she discovered his mob connections. "The problem is," Lois explains, "I can't verify my source. There's no real proof. In fact, I sort of made an 'intuitive leap' to the mob connection." At this point Clark chimes in, "But 'It's not fact unless it's backed,' to quote a certain editor-in-chief." To both reporters' surprise, however, Perry replies, "Print it. You sold *me* on the truth, you'll sell *them*." Under normal circumstances, Perry would never allow Lois to write an investigative piece based on an "intuitive leap," but in a world whimsically redefined by belief, Perry simply accepted Lois's story as true despite the lack of any actual evidence. Eventually the magical lasso is repaired and reality restored, but the entire story illustrates the importance of real truth.[5]

We all recognize that some truths are relative. That is to say, certain "truths" may be true for some people but not for others. For instance, "Superman is the best superhero" is a subjective truth rooted in personal preferences. It's not true for all people in all places. However, as the Justice League discovered, not all truth is relative. Two plus one always equals three. The earth is not flat, and the moon isn't made of green cheese. These are objective truths. They're true for all people regardless of personal opinions or preferences.

So, not *everything* is relative. If that weren't the case, chaos and confusion would run rampant. Instead of buying into a philosophical system that suggests all truth may be shaped by what we believe or experience, our beliefs ought to be shaped by truth. Jesus made a bold assertion when he told Pilate, "I was born and came into the world to testify to the truth. All who love the truth recognize that what I say is true" (John 18:37, NLT). Jesus believed in the reality of truth—truth beyond the subjective and relative, truth grounded in the very character and being of God. Jesus took it upon himself to declare that truth. As seekers of truth, we, like Lois Lane, must make it our mission to discover and discern it.

TRUTH IS REVEALED

As an investigative journalist, Lois's first responsibility is to the truth. In *Superman: Secret Origin* #3, as the *Daily Planet* verges on bankruptcy, Perry bans Lois from writing any exposés that might ruffle the wrong feathers. Lois fights back with the nobility of idealism, shouting, "It's not wrong if it's the truth! Isn't that what the *Daily Planet* stands for? 'Truth, justice, and the American way'! You used to have that hanging on your wall. We're not bankrupt yet, chief. We're here. We need to get the truth out in the open. The truth about everything."[6]

Lois's passion for proclaiming the truth is unparalleled. But the questions remain: How does she determine the truth? How does she sort out fact from fiction? Lois doesn't have the advantage of a magical lasso that compels whomever it binds to tell the truth. Rather, Lois must ferret out the truth the old-fashioned way—through diligence and discernment. The same is true for you and me.

Lois reminds me of the people of Berea. When the early church's leading missionaries, Paul and Silas, arrived in the city of Berea, the residents listened eagerly to Paul's message, and, the Bible says, "They searched the Scriptures day after day to see if Paul and Silas were teaching the truth" (Acts 17:11, NLT). When it came to determining truth, the Bereans knew where to turn.

As Christians, our most trusted source of spiritual truth is God's Word. The Bible is God's divine repository for moral and spiritual truth. Jesus once prayed, "Make them holy by your truth; teach them your word, which is truth" (John 17:17, NLT). The psalmist wrote, "The very essence of your words is truth" (Psalm 119:160, NLT). Paul even refers to Scripture on several occasions as "the word of truth" (Ephesians 1:13; Colossians 1:5; 2 Timothy 2:15). Bottom line: truth is revealed in Scripture.

If we read the Bible diligently, listen to preaching and teaching critically, reflect prayerfully on how the Spirit speaks through biblical texts and faithful teachers as well as in our own hearts and minds, then we are equipped to discern truth as revealed in and through Scripture's witness.

Yet, surprisingly few North American Christians actually read their Bibles. David Nygren once said, "If all the neglected Bibles were dusted off simultaneously, we would have a record dust storm and the sun would be eclipsed for a whole week!"[7] By neglecting God's Word we seriously impair our ability to discern spiritual truth. Televangelists, authors, and media outlets peddle their own take on truth. How do we discern spiritual fact from fiction? The best way to determine whether any particular belief or worldview holds true is to compare it with Scripture. Thus, the more familiar we are with God's Word, the more discerning we become.

Every so often a dishonest dealer tries to pass off a fake or forged comic book as a valuable collectible. Among the most common counterfeits to surface is *Action Comics* #1, which features not only the first appearance of Superman, but also the first appearance of our intrepid reporter, Lois Lane. An authentic copy of the elusive issue fetches more than a million dollars at auction, making it a popular target. But wise consumers can guard against fraud by familiarizing themselves with the real thing. The iconic cover image of Superman hoisting a Studebaker overhead features several unique elements. A white glare appears on the front fender. A yellow running board accents the green car. Beads of sweat fall from the face of the frightened man in the foreground. A short black line floats just below the flying headlight. A falling rock appears on the right edge. No known reprints or reproductions duplicate all of these detection points. A knowledge of the true *Action Comic* #1 helps identify the fakes.

The same is true for discerning truth in our spiritual journey. The more familiar we are with the truth revealed in Scripture, the more quickly we can identify fakes, frauds, and fictions in the flood of information we receive each day.

TRUTH IS REALIZED

Jesus is the realization of truth. In other words, he is the embodiment and personification of truth. The Bible says, "Christ became a human being and lived here on earth among us and was full of loving forgiveness and *truth*" (John 1:14, TLB [italics added]). On the evening before his crucifixion, Jesus told his followers, "I am the way, the *truth*, and the life. No one can come to the Father except through me" (John 14:6, NLT [italics added]).

The question that Pontius Pilate asked on that early morning centuries ago needs to be reconsidered. The Roman governor's quip "What is truth?" overlooks the fact that many things can be true or have truth, but only one thing can actually be the Truth. All truth springs from the person of Jesus. Ironically, Pilate stared Truth in the face and failed to see it. But then, how many times did Lois do the same thing with Superman?

One of the longest-running clichés in comics is how Lois Lane, an award-winning investigative journalist, could sit across the desk from Clark Kent every day and never realize that Clark and Superman are one and the same. In an episode of *Lois & Clark: The New Adventures of Superman* titled "Tempus Fugit," a time-traveling fugitive from the future asks, "Lois, did you know that in the future you are revered at the same level as Superman? There are books about you, statues, an interactive game. You're even a breakfast cereal…. But as much as everybody loves you, there's one question that keeps coming up—how dumb was she?"[8]

Lois and Pilate both demonstrate that it's possible to stare truth in the face and not recognize it. In the comics, when Lois finally discovers Clark's secret identity in *Superman* #53, she wrestles with the realization. "It's not that I'm shocked—actually I'm kind of relieved," she says. "It's like a puzzle that suddenly makes sense because the missing piece is finally in place…. In my heart I think I've known for a long time, but my brain would always dismiss the notion."[9] Lois's words echo the feelings of many when they finally realize the truth about Jesus.

Discovering the truth about Clark and Superman changed everything for Lois and allowed her to experience a new depth of relationship with him. Embracing the truth about Jesus does the same for us. Jesus once told his followers, "You are truly my disciples if you remain faithful to my teachings. And you will know the truth, and the truth will set you free" (John 8:31-32, NLT). Jesus himself is the Truth that sets us free. Knowing him frees us from a life of sin, self-deception, and subjectivism.

***

Not too long ago, several outspoken fans and comic-book creators started a Twitter and Facebook campaign to get Lois Lane her own ongoing comic book series. Now that DC's rebooted universe, *The New 52*, has put Lois and Clark back to square one, it may be a long wait. But fans of Lois can still follow in her footsteps by passionately pursuing the truth. Whether you're an investigative journalist or a follower of Jesus, you can say along with Lois, "The truth is what I'm all about."

NOTES

1. "Ultra Woman," *Lois & Clark: The New Adventures of Superman* (ABC Television, 1995).

2. Jerry Siegel (writer) and Curt Swan (artist), *Superman's Girlfriend, Lois Lane* #21 (DC Comics, 1960).

3. Grant Morrison (writer) and Frank Quitely (artist), *All-Star Superman* #3 (DC Comics, 2005).

4. Mark Schultz (writer) and Yvel Guichet (artist), "The Pantheon," *Superman: The Man of Steel* #126 (DC Comics, 2002).

5. Joe Kelly (writer) and Doug Mahnke (artist), "The Golden Perfect," *Justice League of America* #62–64 (DC Comics, 2002).

6. Geoff Johns (writer) and Gary Frank (artist), *Superman: Secret Origin* #3 (DC Comics, 2010).

7. Robert J. Morgan, *Nelson's Complete Book of Stories, Illustrations, & Quotes* (Nashville: Thomas Nelson, 2000), 62.

8. "Tempus Fugit," *Lois & Clark: The New Adventures of Superman* (ABC Television, 1995).

9. Jerry Ordway (writer/artist), "Truth, Justice, and the American Way," *Superman* #53 (DC Comics, 1991).

3
BLACK WIDOW

A few years ago, if you had whispered the name Black Widow anywhere other than the interior of a comic book store, most people would have assumed that you were talking about a distinctively marked, poisonous arachnid. But thanks to recurring roles in Marvel movies such as *Iron Man 2*, *The Avengers*, and *Captain America: Winter Soldier*, Black Widow is becoming one of the most familiar female superheroes of this decade.

She's also one of my wife's favorite characters to cosplay.

Shortly after Marvel's *The Avengers* shattered box-office records, a local volunteer invited Ashley and me to attend a Relay for Life fundraiser that she dubbed "Bowling with Superheroes." Inspired by the popularity of the Avengers, I attended as Captain America, and Ashley accompanied me as Black Widow. Together we stood outside a small-town bowling alley, waving at passersby and beckoning them to come inside. Some motorists did a double-take as they passed by, while others made U-turns just to get a second look. One elderly couple even pulled over and asked for a picture with us, adding, "Our grandkids are gonna love this!" Inside the brightly decorated bowling alley, we signed autographs and took pictures with kids who came dressed as their own favorite superhero. Fun was had by all, and, of course, the proceeds from that night went to the American Cancer Society.

Ashley has frequently cosplayed as Black Widow ever since.

Black Widow, however, wasn't always a hero. Her past is checkered, to say the least. The Marvel cinematic universe has slowly revealed bits and pieces of her origin. At an early age, Natasha Romanova was enrolled by the KGB into the "Red Room Academy" training program, where she learned combat and espionage skills. Natasha excelled in this strict training environment and soon evolved into a master spy and one of the world's deadliest assassins. Her ruthless effectiveness earned her the code name Black Widow. In Marvel's *The Avengers*, Natasha confesses, "Before I worked for S.H.I.E.L.D., I, uh…Well, I made a name for myself. I have a very specific skill set. I didn't care who I used it for, or on. I got on S.H.I.E.L.D.'s radar in a bad way. Agent Barton was sent to kill me. He made a different call."[1]

Agent Barton, also known as Hawkeye, saw potential in Natasha and disobeyed his orders. At Barton's behest, Nick Fury, the director of S.H.I.E.L.D. (Strategic Homeland Intervention Espionage and Logistics Division), made Natasha an irresistible offer. He would wipe her record clean if she would join S.H.I.E.L.D. and work for the good guys.

This became the defining moment for Black Widow. Given a fresh start and a clean slate, Natasha put her combat and espionage skills to use for the greater good. Hands once soaked in innocent blood became instruments of freedom and justice. Her heroism even earned her a place on the Avengers roster, where she now defends the world from super-powered villains and alien invasions.

Natasha's story resonates with those whose lives are changed dramatically by an encounter with Jesus Christ. The apostle Paul knew all about that. While his life is detailed in the New Testament book of Acts, Paul himself concisely related the essential elements of his story while on trial before King Agrippa (Acts 26:1-24). The stories of both Black Widow and Paul separate neatly into three segments, each beginning with past sin.

OUR SIN

After years of working as a mercenary and paid assassin, Black Widow was well aware of her moral faults and failures. In a revealing scene from *Marvel's The Avengers*, Black Widow is sent to interrogate Thor's mischievous brother, Loki. Baiting Loki into letting his guard down, Widow confesses, "I've got red in my ledger. I'd like to wipe it out." With a malicious tone, Loki replies, "Can you? Can you wipe out that much red? Drakov's daughter, Sao Paulo, the hospital fire?…Your ledger is dripping, it's gushing red…. You lie and kill in the service of liars and killers."[2]

Like Black Widow, the apostle Paul had red in his ledger as well. Trained from an early age in the Hebrew Scriptures, Paul missed the mark when his devout and (self-)righteous Jewish faith came face to face with the disciples of Jesus. In his own words, Paul describes his transgressions this way:

> I used to believe that I ought to do everything I could to oppose the very name of Jesus the Nazarene. Indeed, I did just that in Jerusalem. Authorized by the leading priests, I caused many believers there to be sent to prison. And I cast my vote against them when they were condemned to death. Many times I had them punished in the synagogues to get them to curse Jesus. I was so violently opposed to them that I even chased them down in foreign cities. (Acts 26:9-11, NLT)

For years, the man born as Saul was a great threat to early Christianity. Bankrolled by Jerusalem's religious leaders, he passionately pursued Christ-followers from one city to another, flogging them until they renounced their faith in Jesus. Those who remained firm in their faith he sent to prison—or worse. To be fair, he doesn't confess to killing anyone himself; he stepped aside and let his minions bloody their hands instead.

Few readers of this chapter have committed crimes as violent as Natasha's or as vengeful as Saul/Paul's. Yet, like them, our past is swarming with sins. *Sin* is the Bible's word for everything that isn't good and right in relationship with God, other people, creation, and self. We may not be spies, assassins, or persecutors of the church, but we are all sinners. The Bible assures us of this: "For everyone has sinned; we all fall short of God's glorious standard" (Romans 3:23, NLT). What is God's glorious standard? You're probably familiar with the Ten Commandments. Do a simple exercise with me. Compare your life to these three standards from the Ten Commandments:

1. "You shall not steal." Have you ever stolen anything? A paper clip? A peanut? That makes you a thief.

2. "You shall not lie." Anyone who says they haven't, just did.

3. "You shall not kill." Before you excuse yourself from this one, remember that Jesus once said, "You have heard that our ancestors were told, 'You must not murder. If you commit murder, you are subject to judgment.' But I say, if you are even angry with someone, you are subject to judgment!" (Matthew 5:21-22, NLT).

If you're like me, you didn't score very well. We're all lying, thieving, killers at heart. And that's just three out of ten. We could keep going, but I don't think we'd fare any better. Besides, God's standard is even more glorious than the Ten Commandments. Right smack in the middle of the Sermon on the Mount, Jesus sets the bar: "You are to be perfect, even as your Father in heaven is perfect" (Matthew 5:48, NLT). If you compare yourself to Paul in his "Saul" days or to Natasha Romanov, you might look pretty good. But God's standard is *God*. None of us can meet God's glorious standard because none of us is perfect. We all fall short.

Like Natasha, we each have red in our ledgers, and left to ourselves, not one of us is able to wipe it out. We need to look elsewhere for our salvation.

OUR SALVATION

Natasha Romanova had a life-changing experience when she met Nick Fury. In a scene only alluded to in the films and comics, I imagine Fury entering a cold, sterile interrogation room and slapping a two-inch thick file on the table before Natasha—a file brimming with her every misdemeanor, felony, and infraction. She was guilty; her ledger was dripping, gushing red. But rather than condemning her for her crimes, the director of S.H.I.E.L.D. extends an offer of forgiveness: "I can make it all go away."

What Nick Fury did for Black Widow, Jesus did for Paul. As he addressed King Agrippa, Paul recalled a particular day in his career as a persecutor of Jesus' disciples:

> I was on such a mission to Damascus, armed with the authority and commission of the leading priests. About noon, Your Majesty, as I was on the road, a light from heaven brighter than the sun shone down on me and my companions. We all fell down, and I heard a voice saying to me in Aramaic, "Saul, Saul, why are you persecuting me? It is useless for you to fight against my will."
>
> "Who are you, lord?" I asked.
>
> And the Lord replied, "I am Jesus." (Acts 26:12-15, NLT)

Knees pressed into the pavement, surrounded by heaven's light, Saul encountered the risen Jesus and everything changed—including his name.

Unlike Nick Fury, Jesus didn't merely close the file on our sins and mark it "classified." He took it to the cross with him and nailed it there. The Bible says that Jesus "personally carried our sins in his body on the cross so that we can be dead to sin and live for what is right. By his wounds you are healed" (1 Peter 2:24, NLT). All our faults, failures, and foibles went with Jesus to the cross— the selfishness of the glutton, the bitterness of the angry, the shame of the adulterer. Jesus took it all, as if he had lied or cheated or cursed his Maker.

After six hours of agony upon the cross, Jesus whispered, "It is finished!" (John 19:30). What makes these words so meaningful is that the Greek word translated "it is finished" is *tetelestai*, an accounting term that means "paid in full." When Jesus uttered those words, he wiped out all the red in my ledger and yours. He paid the debt that we could never pay.

Of course, forgiveness—both for Natasha and Saul—was only the beginning. From that point on each of them entered into a life of service.

OUR SERVICE

After accepting Nick Fury's offer and joining S.H.I.E.L.D., Black Widow began putting her skills to better use. In *Captain America: The Winter Soldier*, she remembers an early assignment. "Five years ago," she recalls, "I was escorting a nuclear engineer out of Iran, somebody shot at my tires near Odessa. We lost control, went straight over a cliff. I pulled us out, but the Winter Soldier was there. I was covering my engineer, so he shot him straight through me."[3] Her service to S.H.I.E.L.D. turned Natasha's life completely around, so much so that she willingly took a bullet from a mysterious assassin to protect an innocent man. Rather than taking lives, she protected life.

Just as Nick Fury enlisted Black Widow into the service of S.H.I.E.L.D., Jesus drafted Paul into the service of God's kingdom.

Standing before the king, Paul drew his story to close by recounting Jesus' words to him: "Now get to your feet! For I have appeared to you to appoint you as my servant and witness. Tell people that you have seen me, and tell them what I will show you in the future" (Acts 26:16, NLT).

Paul's change was no less dramatic than Natasha's. From that day forward, Paul lived his life for Jesus. He told everyone whom he encountered what Jesus had done for him. He became an ambassador of God's love, teaching others to love their neighbor and even to love their enemies. Paul became one of Christianity's first missionaries, traveling all across the ancient world, building churches and changing lives.

Not all of us are called to be a missionary (or an agent of S.H.I.E.L.D., for that matter), but when you embrace Jesus as your Savior, he essentially tells you, "Now get to your feet! We have work to do." He calls every believer into a life of service marked by a love for God, pursuit of justice, and acts of kindness and mercy. Jesus once said, "Your attitude must be like my own, for I, the Messiah, did not come to be served, but to serve, and to give my life as a ransom for many" (Matthew 20:28, TLB).

Serving and giving ought to define your life as well. Opportunities for service abound. Teaching a Sunday school class, providing disaster relief for tornado-ravaged towns, feeding the hungry in war-torn nations, or raising awareness about global sex trafficking are just a fraction of the ways Christians serve Jesus. But one of the simplest and most essential means of serving Jesus is telling others about him. That's what Paul did. On numerous occasions throughout Scripture, Paul shared the story of how he came to Christ, just as he did with King Agrippa in Acts 26.

Sharing your own salvation story is an essential part of serving Jesus. You may not be a Bible scholar or apologist, but you are an authority on your own life. Many people who won't accept the authority of the Bible will listen to an honest personal story. By sharing the story of how you came to faith in Christ, you build a bridge that Jesus can walk across from your heart to someone else's.

* * *

Perhaps you can identify with Paul and relate to Natasha. Certainly we have all sinned and fallen short, just they did. But Someone has stepped in, paid the debt of your sin, and washed the red from your ledger. Jesus has offered you salvation and called you to service. If you accept his offer, it will change *your* life.

NOTES

1. *Marvel's The Avengers*, directed by Joss Whedon (Walt Disney Studios, 2012).

2. Ibid.

3. *Captain America: The Winter Soldier*, directed by Anthony Russo and Joe Russo (Walt Disney Studios, 2014).

4
BATMAN

Doesn't everyone know the story of Batman? Once you've heard it, you can never forget it. As a young boy, Bruce Wayne excitedly emerged from a theater in Gotham City along with his wealthy socialite parents, Thomas and Martha. But, as the trio made their way through a dimly lit alley, a mugger stepped out of the shadows, waving a gun and demanding money. Before the couple could comply, the thief pulled the trigger. Bruce watched in horror as his parents were killed in front of him.

Days later, kneeling by his bedside, Bruce solemnly vowed to avenge his parents' death by waging war on criminals. Relying on his billion-dollar inheritance, Bruce traveled abroad, studying under the greatest criminologists, detectives, and martial artists in the world. When he finally returned home to Gotham City, he adopted a persona that strikes fear into the hearts of criminals— the Batman.

But what starts off as one man's war on crime quickly turns into a family affair. While attending the circus, Bruce witnessed the murder of a husband-and-wife trapeze team. Their son and fellow acrobat, Dick Grayson, watched in frozen fear as they fell to their deaths from the top of the tent. Bruce adopted the orphaned boy and trained him to become Batman's sidekick—Robin.

In time, Dick Grayson grew up, started calling himself Nightwing, and a new Robin filled his tights. Several Robins have come and gone over the years, and many other heroes have joined Batman's cadre of crime fighters—including Huntress, Oracle, Azrael, more than one Batgirl, Batwoman, Catwoman, Alfred, and even Ace the Bat-Hound! Ironically, the world's bravest loner has comics' largest extended family.

This is what makes Batman such a fun character to cosplay for my family. I'm always searching for a team or family of superheroes to accommodate our family of five, rather than mixing and matching a collection of random heroes.

After taking my first foray into costuming as Superman, I knew that Batman would be my next project. I had sharpened my sewing skills and worked out the kinks in creating Superman costumes, so when Halloween of 2009 rolled around, I worked hard to outfit everyone in our family with a Batman-themed costume.

I created a classic blue and grey Batman for myself, a Batgirl costume for my wife, and a Robin for my son. By the time those three were finished, Halloween was fast approaching, so I cheated and bought off-the-shelf costumes for my two girls, who were still in diapers. We debuted these costumes at a Trunk-or-Treat event with our small-town church. Members parked their cars and decorated their trunks as kids from all over the neighborhood clamored to see Batman and his supporting cast handing out candy in front of our church building. We drew quite a crowd and gave away oodles of candy along with dozens of gospel tracts and invitations to church.

Since then we've done multiple other versions of these and other bat-related characters. Batman, Robin, and the rest of the gang are consistently among the most popular superheroes to portray among cosplayers.

So, what spiritual truth does the Caped Crusader illustrate?

Batman's persistent pursuit of partners is a vivid reminder that you and I were formed for God's family. The loss of his biological family drove Bruce Wayne to build the largest crime-fighting family in comic books—a family that he relies upon for support, strength, and stability in his war on crime. That's what the church provides for you and me.

All of us need a place to belong. All of us need to be part of something bigger than ourselves. All of us need to experience family and fellowship. Going to church is not primarily about worship. You can worship God at home from the comfort of your recliner, or behind the wheel of your car, or while kneeling at your bedside. Church is primarily about family. The Bible uses a lot of metaphors to describe the church, but the most persistent is family. In the New Testament, believers call one another "brother" and "sister." The Bible describes our "adoption" as children of God (Romans 8:14-15). The church is called the "household" of God. The Bible says, "Now you…are not foreigners or strangers any longer, but are citizens together with God's holy people. You belong to God's family" (Ephesians 2:19, NCV).

Maybe there's a pew in your home church worn in the shape of your bottom. Maybe you're as comfortable in your church family as you are in your favorite pajamas. On the other hand, maybe it's been a while since you darkened a church doorstep. Maybe you've never felt the blessing of belonging to something as big as the family of God. Either way, I'd like to share with you something that Scripture teaches us about the benefits of family and fellowship:

> Two are better than one, because they have a good return for their labor: If either of them falls down, one can help the other up. But pity anyone who falls and has no one to help them up. Also, if two lie down together, they will keep warm. But how can one keep warm alone? Though one may be overpowered, two can defend themselves. A cord of three strands is not quickly broken. (Ecclesiastes 4:9-12, NIV)

In legendary wisdom, the Teacher in the book of Ecclesiastes says, "Two people are better than one." Batman certainly would agree. His story illustrates three benefits of belonging to an extended, adoptive family, which is exactly what the church can be. First, Batman demonstrates that a family can provide strength.

STRENGTH

Bruce Wayne learned as a child the pain of being alone, and early on in his superhero career he discovered a principle that holds true for every epoch of time: there's strength in numbers. None of us can do alone what all of us can do together.

Batman embraced this principle by training young protégées like Robin and Batgirl. But he really elevates his war on crime in a comic series titled *Batman Incorporated* by essentially "franchising" his name. Bruce scours the planet for the best of the best, drafting, training, and commanding a global team of heroes who will answer to Batman himself. A worldwide team of caped crusaders fights crime in major cities all over the world because Batman recognized the power of teamwork.

In an old *Peanuts* comic strip, Lucy strolls into the room and demands that her brother, Linus, change TV channels. "What makes you think you can just walk right in here and take over?" asks Linus. "These five fingers," says Lucy. "Individually they are nothing, but when I curl them together like this into a single unit, they form a weapon that is terrible to behold." Linus sighs, "Which channel do you want?" Then turning away, he looks at his own fingers and asks, "Why can't you guys get organized like that?"[1] For better or worse, that's the power of teamwork!

Just as Batman's superhero family provided him with the power of a team, belonging to a church family provides God's people with similar strength. Notice these verses again from another translation: "Two people are better than one, because they get more done by working together…. A rope that is woven of three strings is hard to break" (Ecclesiastes 4:9,12, NCV). Whether you are interested in serving your community by providing meals for the needy, or sharing God's love by giving away free fuel at your local gas station, or sharing the message of Christ by handing out copies of the gospel at comic book conventions, you'll always make a bigger impact if you work as part of a team. None of us can do everything, but all of us can do something. And none of us can do alone what all of us can do together.

That's the first reason God gave us the church. Another reason, and another benefit of belonging to a family illustrated by Batman, is support.

SUPPORT

Belonging to a family provides support. In one of my favorite Batman stories, a graphic novel titled *Hush* by Jeph Loeb and Jim Lee, the story opens with Batman chasing down the feline thief, Catwoman. With acrobatic agility, Batman swings from rooftop to rooftop until his grappling hook suddenly snaps. As the concrete below rushes ever closer, Batman lurches toward a stone gargoyle in hopes of breaking his fall. Instead, the abrupt strain breaks both his shoulder and the statue, sending Batman crashing into a darkened alley—Crime Alley. Crippled and unconscious in the most dangerous neighborhood in Gotham, the Dark Knight is slowly surrounded by a cowardly and superstitious lot of criminals and lowlifes.

Thankfully, Oracle was monitoring Batman from the safety of her computer console and quickly calls for help. Answering the call, the Huntress leaps to Batman's rescue, helps him to his feet, and returns him to the Batmobile. The scene closes with a shadowy figure overlooking the alley, whispering the words of Aristotle: "Without friends no one would choose to live, though he had all other goods."[2]

Of course, your grappling hook doesn't have to snap while you're swinging above the city for you to experience a fall. We all stumble from time to time. Maybe you've just been through a bad breakup, maybe you've lost your job, maybe you've fallen prey to an addiction that you thought you'd beaten. Your troubles may be different from mine, but we all have them.

The Teacher put it this way: "Two are better off than one, because they can work more effectively. If one of them falls down, the other can help him up. But if someone is alone and falls, it's just too bad, because there is no one to help him" (Ecclesiastes 4:9-10, GNB).

In a *Calvin and Hobbes* comic strip, Calvin crawls out of bed, dresses in his new school clothes, and heads out the door. During the day, he sits on some bubble gum, gets beat up by a bully, fails a test, and gets rained on. At bedtime he says, "You know, Hobbes, some days even my lucky rocketship underpants don't help."[3]

We all have days like that. Jesus warned that we would. "In this world you will have trouble," he said (John 16:33, NIV). We all have burdens to bear and bad days to endure, and some days even wearing your lucky underpants won't help! But belonging to a church family that cares about you and lifts you up whenever you fall—that does help. The Bible says, "Help carry each other's burdens. In this way you will follow Christ's teachings" (Galatians 6:2, GW). Batman's extended family strengthened and supported him, and our church family can do the same for us.

STIRRING

Finally, belonging to a family stirs us up—that is, it motivates and encourages us. The Warner Brothers cartoon series *Batman Beyond* (originally aired 1999–2001) revisits a much older Bruce Wayne. After his many years of service, Batman turns his back on the city that he swore to protect and shrouds himself from society in the dark shadows of his hollow mansion. Alfred is gone, and all Bruce's other partners in crime fighting went their separate ways.

Aging and alone, Bruce gave up on his mission and abandoned the vow he made at his bedside all those years ago. That is, until Terry McGuiness accidentally uncovers Bruce's secret entrance to the Bat Cave. Terry's persistence and mere presence stirs the coals in Bruce's heart, prompting him to come out of retirement and train Terry to take on the mantle of the Bat.[4]

Similarly, any time one of God's children gets separated from the family, our fire fades. Our spirits grow cold. The Bible says, "And let us consider how to stir up one another to love and good works, not neglecting to meet together, as is the habit of some, but encouraging one another" (Hebrews 10:24-25, ESV). One of the most important reasons the church meets together every Sunday is to stir each other up and encourage each other.

As the Teacher in Ecclesiastes said, "Two people are better off than one, for...two people lying close together can keep each other warm. But how can one be warm alone?" (Ecclesiastes 4:9-11, NLT). While this is practical advice for a nomadic people living in the desert, it also serves as a spiritual metaphor. You don't have to live in a tent in the tundra to feel cold and alone.

A pastor once visited a man who had been absent from church for some time. When the pastor arrived at the house of his wayward parishioner, he found him sitting by a fire of glowing coals. The man fully expected his pastor to rebuke him for his lack of attendance. Instead, the pastor drew up a chair beside the fireplace. He reached into the fire with metal tongs, removed one of the red glowing coals, and placed it by itself on the hearth. In no time at all, the coal lost its glow and moments later it was cold and grey. Looking up into the face of his pastor who hadn't spoken a word, the man said, "I'll be there next Sunday." That parishioner understood what the writer of Ecclesiastes asserted.

The warmth that you feel in your heart as you worship alongside fellow believers? That's your coals being stirred. It's your passion for Jesus—your love for God and for people—being rekindled.

When you first gave your heart to Jesus, he lit a fire in your soul. Belonging to a church family fans the flames and keeps you spiritually warm.

***

Batman may be the world's greatest detective and one of DC Comics's most iconic heroes, but even he doesn't do it alone. Likewise, God doesn't just call us to believe; God calls us to belong. The entire Bible is the story of God building a family that will support, strengthen, and stir one another up to love and good works for all eternity. God created you to be a part of that family.

NOTES

1. Charles M. Schulz, *Peanuts*, January 6, 1964 (available online: http://www.peanuts.com/search/?keyword=fingers&type=comic_strips&cpage=2#.VmbnZIQ4lOI).

2. Jeph Loeb (writer) and Jim Lee (artist), *Hush* (DC Comics, 2009).

3. Bill Watterson, *Calvin and Hobbes* (available online: http://thecuriousbrain.com/?p=25422).

4. "Rebirth," *Batman Beyond*, Jan 1999 (The WB Television, 1999).

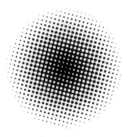

THE BAYLES FAMILY COSPLAYS AS THE 1980s COMIC-BOOK VERSION OF MARVEL'S FANTASTIC FOUR!

PHOTO BY FRIENDLY BYSTANDER

5
FANTASTIC FOUR

In the last chapter we saw how Batman, along with his many crime-fighting companions, illustrates the benefits of belonging to a church family. However, families don't always get along. That's where the Fantastic Four come in. The Fantastic Four, also known as the First Family of Marvel Comics, have a rich and interesting origin.

Stan Lee came to work for Marvel Comics back in 1939 and eventually worked his way up the ladder to become the editor-in-chief. For decades, however, Marvel's only successful title figure was Captain America, and the company struggled to compete with DC Comics's much more popular characters—Superman, Batman, and Wonder Woman. Stan was about to call it quits when his wife urged him to create a new team of characters that he found interesting—characters that he could relate to personally. Prior to this, most superheroes were idealistically perfect people with no serious, lasting problems, and who always got along with one another. So in 1961, acting on his wife's advice, Stan Lee created a team of superheroes who were flawed, imperfect, and even argumentative.

Their story began with the inaugural test flight of a space shuttle designed by Reed Richards, one of the world's foremost scientific minds. During the mission, cosmic rays bombarded the ship and forced it to crash land back on earth, where Reed, his then-girlfriend Sue Storm, her brother Johnny Storm, and test pilot Ben Grimm emerged from the wreckage to discover they had been miraculously endowed with fantastic abilities. Reed became the super-stretchy Mr. Fantastic. Ben transformed into the "ever-lovin' blue-eyed" Thing. Sue turned transparent and chose the codename Invisible Girl. And Johnny burst into flames as the Human Torch. Together they formed the Fantastic Four!

Stan Lee's new team experienced tremendous popularity, which spurred Stan to create a veritable parade of flawed new heroes, including Iron Man, Thor, Hulk, the X-Men, and Spider-Man. This resurgence of creativity and popularity became known as the Marvel Age of Comics, and Marvel Comics has consistently outsold DC Comics ever since.

It's undoubtedly the dynamic among the members of the Fantastic Four that has made them such a fan-favorite and why my family and I enjoy cosplaying them so much. They're a family, biologically in part but by "adoption" as well. They love one another to death—and it just might come to that!

So, if the Bat family illustrates the benefits of belonging to a family, the Fantastic Four illustrate the difficulties. Every church, just like every family, experiences conflict. Personalities clash. Feelings get hurt. People hold grudges. No church is perfect, because every church consists of imperfect people. And yet, the Bible says, "You should be like one big happy family, full of sympathy toward each other, loving one another with tender hearts and humble minds" (1 Peter 3:8, TLB). Of course, that's a lot easier said than done. An old rhyme puts it this way:

> What joy to love the saints above
> When I get home to glory.
> To love below, the saints I know,
> Well, that's another story!

All people—including Christians—can be downright unlovable at times. We can be selfish, stubborn, and short-sighted. Thankfully, the Fantastic Four remind us of some important spiritual lessons when it comes to getting along with the person in the pew beside you.

BE PITIFUL

Unlike the other members of the Fantastic Four who still look normal after being exposed to the cosmic radiation, Ben's skin transforms into a thick, rocky, orange hide. Trapped in his monstrous form, Ben is a rock-solid yet unhappy member of the team, and he evolves a personality to match his stony exterior. Ben gets angry at the world because of how people react to his appearance, and he harbors a grudge against his best friend, Reed Richards, for causing the accident that resulted in his transformation.

In Fox's 2005 film *Fantastic Four*, Ben returns to his fiancée, Debbie, after the accident, hoping to find unconditional love and acceptance. Instead, horrified by his appearance, Debbie screams in fright and returns his ring. Ben then spends the night alone on the Brooklyn Bridge. When a seemingly suicidal man prepares to jump off the bridge, Ben calls out, "Hey pal, you think you got problems? Take a good look [at me]." Later, in the same film, Ben attempts to drown his sorrows at a local tavern. But when he tries lifting his drink, his strong stony hands shatter the glass. "If there is a God," Ben muses, "he hates me."[1]

It's hard not to feel bad for Ben. Beneath Ben's stony skin is a tender heart. Because of his appearance, he doesn't fit in with the rest of the world. He's marginalized and alienated. As a result, he's left with a big orange chip on his shoulder, always looking for someone to clobber!

While they might not look gravelly and orange on the outside, many Ben Grimms occupy church pews all around the world. They tend to be grumpy and rough around the edges. Cranky and cantankerous, their gruff exteriors often rub people the wrong way, but beneath the surface might lay tender hearts. This is why Peter instructs Christians, "Be pitiful" (1 Peter 3:8, KJV). The word *pitiful* usually has a negative connotation in our day, but in the Bible it refers to being full of pity toward others. The dictionary defines pity as "sympathetic or kindly sorrow evoked by the suffering, distress, or misfortune of another, often leading one to give relief or aid or to show mercy."[2] This is what Peter had in mind when he encouraged church members to "be pitiful." He wants us to understand and empathize with the suffering and misfortune of our brothers and sisters in Christ.

We know all about the Thing's misfortune because we can read the comics or watch the cartoons. But when it comes to the people with whom we share a pew, we often have no way of knowing what struggles or sorrows they've faced. The grumpy old guy in the back pew may be carrying a lifetime of regrets. The short-tempered woman who cut in front of you to get a cup of coffee may have spent the night in the hospital watching her mother fade away. The teenage girl who seems standoffish may have been rejected so often that she's too afraid to open up.

When someone's dealt a difficult hand, it often results in a stony surface. That's why the Bible instructs us to be tenderhearted, to sympathize with each other, and to love each other as brothers and sisters. In other words, "be pitiful." That's the first key in overcoming conflict that we learn from the Fantastic Four. The Human Torch illustrates another one.

BE PATIENT

Still young and rebellious, keeping a cool head was never one of Johnny Storm's strong suits. The archetypal hothead of the group, Johnny often makes brash decisions and disobeys direct orders. In a later scene from Fox's 2005 movie, Reed requests that the entire team confine themselves to the Baxter Building, home of Reed's laboratory, while he studies the effects of the cosmic cloud on their DNA. While the rest of the team complies with the quarantine, Johnny impulsively blows off Reed's wishes and shows up at a nationally televised motorbike competition, where he makes a spectacle of himself and his newfound powers. After the competition, a reporter asks Johnny about each member of the team, including Ben. "What is that? What do you call that thing?" she asks. "That's it," Johnny replies, "the Thing!"

When Ben sees the interview on television, his feelings are hurt, and he growls, "Okay, now I'm gonna kill him." He retaliates by tracking Johnny down and smashing his shiny new sports car, crumpling it into a twisted ball of rubber and steel. The situation only escalates from there. When Johnny sees what Ben did to his car, he snaps back, "You think that's funny, Pebbles?" Then he launches a couple of fireballs at Ben's face before Ben responds with a punch that sends Johnny sailing into a mobile billboard.

Sadly, this kind of behavior is all too common for the Fantastic Four—at least for Johnny and Ben. What's worse, this kind of behavior is all too common in the church. That's why Peter continues, "Don't repay evil for evil. Don't retaliate with insults when people insult you. Instead, pay them back with a blessing. That is what God has called you to do, and he will grant you his blessing" (1 Peter 3:9, NLT). The Old Testament says, "A hot-tempered person starts fights; a cool-tempered person stops them" (Proverbs 15:18, NLT). The best response to being hurt or insulted by another person is not payback, but patience.

The Greek word for *patience* offers an illustration to which the Human Torch could relate well. It literally meant "taking a long time to boil." Picture a pot of water on the stove. The water boils quickly when the flame is high. It takes a long time if the flame is low. Patience doesn't ignore evil or insults; rather, patience simply keeps the flame low.

When people offend you or hurt your feelings, instead of lashing out in retaliation, be patient. Keep the flame low. Then calmly let them know how much they mean to you and how you feel. In so doing, you'll pay them back with a blessing. Chances are they never meant to hurt you anyway. But even if they did, God has called you to be a blessing to them, and the Lord will bless you in return.

BE PEACEABLE

In the car-crunching movie scene mentioned earlier, when tempers flared and fists flew, Sue Storm stepped in. "Wait a minute, guys," Sue pleads. "Johnny, say you're sorry," she insists. "Ben, don't do this," she demands. When her words fall on deaf ears, Sue steps between the two tussling teammates and pushes them apart with one of her force fields. Not content to simply stop the fight, Sue follows Ben as he sulks away and attempts to mediate. "Wait, Ben. Slow down. He didn't mean it. You know Johnny. He's always been a hothead," Sue admits. Then she reminds the big orange guy, "We're all in this together, Ben."

In his closing comments about handling hot tempers and cold shoulders, Peter quotes from the psalms, saying, "If you want to enjoy life and see more happy days,… Search for peace, and work to maintain it" (1 Peter 3:10-11, NLT). That has often been Sue's role on the team—peacemaker. She frequently encourages her teammates to talk things out, settle their disputes, and make amends. I think that we could all stand to be a little more like Sue Storm. As peacemaker, Sue changes the whole climate of whatever situation she finds herself in.

I think that there are essentially two types of personalities. There are "thermostat" people and there are "thermometer" people. A thermometer reflects the climate of the room. If the room is cold, it's cold. If the temperature gets hot, the thermometer gets hot too. A thermostat, on the other hand, can change the climate of the room. By adjusting its setting, a thermostat can change a cold room into one that's warm, or a hot room into one that's cool. A peacemaker is a thermostat person. A peacemaker can change the climate of whatever room he or she is in. Have you ever seen that happen? Have you ever been in a room where everybody is negative and complaining, and everything is going wrong? Then a thermostat person enters the room with a cool head and a warm heart, and suddenly the whole climate changes.

Like Peter said, we need to "search for peace, and work to maintain it" (1 Peter 3:11, NLT). God wants peacemakers in the church. God wants peacemakers in the workplace. God wants peacemakers out in the world—people who never dwell on the negative, but concentrate on the positive, people who seek peace and work to maintain it. It takes a lot of spiritual maturity to be that kind of person. But the more we allow God's Spirit to work inside of us, the less hardheaded and hardhearted we'll be and the more pitiful, patient, and peaceable we'll become.

***

The Fantastic Four have their skirmishes and squabbles, but they are one of the most enduring and adored teams in comic book history. They've been around for over fifty years, they're still together, still saving the world, and not even Doctor Doom could tear them apart!

Belonging to God's family is a precious gift. We all need a family that will pity—that is, love—us even when we're unpleasant, forgive us when we lose our patience, and help us to live at peace with everyone. That's the kind of family the Fantastic Four is for Reed, Sue, Johnny, and Ben. And that's what church can be for you and me.

NOTES
1. *Fantastic Four*, directed by Tim Story (20th Century Fox, 2005).
2. Dictionary.com, "Pity," http://dictionary.reference.com/ browse /pity?s=t.

6
GREEN LANTERN

Hal Jordan, a cocky test pilot for Ferris Aircraft, performed a routine flight simulator run when a mysterious green energy suddenly enveloped his capsule, ripping it from the platform and carrying it off into the desert hundreds of miles west. Jordan emerged from the simulator to discover a downed spacecraft and a dying purple alien named Abin Sur. With his last breath Abin Sur explains, "I am the Green Lantern of space sector 2814. I am dying. You have been chosen to be my successor."[1]

The Green Lanterns are intergalactic peacekeepers commissioned by an immortal race of little blue aliens. These immortals, the Guardians, built a world from where they could watch over all of existence, the planet Oa. They then divided the universe into 3,600 sectors and sent a ring powered by the energy of will to every sector of the universe to select a recruit. These recruits form the Green Lantern Corps.

With thousands of Lanterns to choose from—both male and female, humanoid and alien—the size and diversity of the Green Lantern Corps allows for endless variety and imagination in costuming. Our family first cosplayed as Green Lanterns for a local Halloween Parade in Carlinville, Illinois. We'd been living in the area for only a few months, and no one bothered to tell us that adults don't normally dress up for the parade. Needless to say, we attracted plenty of attention in our green and black spandex outfits. I custom-tailored each of our five costumes, some based on the animated series incarnations and others adapted from the comic books. Sadly, the general public isn't as familiar with Green Lantern as they are with more notable superheroes, like Spider-Man or Batman. Few people recognized our costumes. Some even thought that we were the Power Rangers. So when asked (repeatedly), I would point to the glowing green power ring adorning my finger and say, "I'm Green Lantern."

The ring itself is the source of a Green Lantern's power, and when a Green Lantern dies, the ring follows its programming to seek out a worthy successor. Upon finding a new recruit, the ring announces, "You have the ability to overcome great fear. Welcome to the Green Lantern Corps."

I find this intriguing. The ring didn't choose Hal Jordan because of his strong moral character, his heroic nature, or even his creativity. No, the only stipulation for becoming a Green Lantern is the ability to overcome great fear. In the graphic novel *Green Lantern: Secret Origin*, Abin Sur underscored this with his dying words: "You have been chosen for one reason. You are a man who can overcome great fear."[2] If you think about it, though, that is quite an ability.

If there is one great enemy of faith, it's fear. In the 2011 movie, fellow Green Lantern Sinestro describes the paralyzing effects of fear to Hal Jordan during a training session: "Fear is the enemy. Fear is what stops you, and makes you weak. When you're afraid, you can't act. You can't act, you can't defend. You can't defend, you die!"[3] Fear has the same effect on our faith.

What's your worst fear? In 1997, the Sunday supplement magazine *USA Weekend* ran a cover story entitled "Fear: What Americans Are Afraid of Today."[4] In a scientific poll, the magazine uncovered the things that U.S. residents fear most. The majority feared being in a car crash or getting diagnosed with cancer. Half of those surveyed feared inadequate retirement funds and having too much month left at the end of the money. A third of Americans were afraid of getting Alzheimer's, food poisoning, or being the victim of violence. Of course, the list goes on. You might have a fear of failure or rejection or public embarrassment. Maybe you're afraid of being abused, abandoned, or alone. Every sunrise brings fresh reasons for fear. Some of us can sympathize with the *Peanuts* character Charlie Brown when he said, "I've developed a new philosophy. I only dread one day at time."[5]

Wouldn't it be great if you and I had the ability to overcome great fear?

God takes our fears seriously and wants us to overcome them. In fact, the Bible contains no fewer than 366 commands to "not be afraid" or "fear not" or "have courage." That's one for every day of the year, including Leap Year. Of the 125 commands that Jesus gave in the New Testament, the one he repeated the most is the phrase "Don't be afraid." Since Jesus orders us so often not to be afraid, surely he also gives us the ability to obey him — to overcome our fears. So how do you and I overcome great fear?

Twelve disciples stuck in a leaky fishing boat on the Sea of Galilee may have wondered the same thing. The sky rumbled above them, the water churned beneath them. The Bible says, "Suddenly, a fierce storm struck the lake, with waves breaking into the boat" (Matthew 8:24, NLT). Their tiny ship was tossed and spun on the whitecaps of angry waves like the Minnow from the TV series *Gilligan's Island*. These rough and tough sailors feared for their lives. Trembling and terrified, one of them shouted over the crashing waves, "Lord, save us! We're going to drown!" (Matthew 8:25, NLT). Steadily, Jesus responded, "Why are you afraid? You have so little faith!" (Matthew 8:26, NLT).

Faith, Jesus seems to say, is the antithesis of fear. Faith and fear can't exist in the same heart at the same time. Do you want less fear in your life? The answer is more faith. Wouldn't it be wonderful if faith, not fear, was your instinctive response to danger? Both Green Lantern and Jesus' disciples reveal three reasons we can respond in faith rather than fear, regardless of our situation or circumstances.

PERSPECTIVE

When calamity, catastrophe, or cataclysm befall us—whether by means of death, divorce, disease, terrorism, or tornadoes—we're left wondering why. *Why* God? *Why* me? *Why*?

Hal Jordan once posed the same question to the Guardians of Oa in *Green Lantern: Secret Origin*. Surrounded by a panel of little blue aliens with unkempt hair and long red robes, the rookie Green Lantern had the audacity to challenge their authority and wisdom. "Why?" he asked. A Guardian named Ganthet responded with both confidence and compassion, "We have lived for billions of years. What we do, we do for the well-being of the entire universe."[6]

Being eons old gave the Guardians a grander perspective of the universe and each person's role in it. The same is true of God. God isn't just old; God is eternal and infinite in wisdom and knowledge. And Jesus is very much his heavenly Father's son.

In the Gospel story about Jesus calming the storm, Mark's account includes a small detail that Matthew doesn't record in his retelling. Mark notes, "As evening came, Jesus said to his disciples, 'Let's cross to the other side of the lake'" (Mark 4:35, NLT). The eye absorbs this sentence in a moment, then moves on to the next. But this simple statement shows that *Jesus* planned to set sail that day. Peter, James, John and the rest were simply following where he led.

So the question is this: did Jesus know that the storm was coming? The Bible doesn't answer that, but I'm betting that Jesus knew full well that a storm was setting in. Being fully God, he had that heavenly perspective. And it was within his power to prevent it or avoid it. Instead, he traveled with them into the storm.

Following Jesus doesn't guarantee smooth sailing. Christians develop cancer, file for bankruptcy, battle addictions, and experience unemployment, and, as a result, we face fears. But we can overcome whatever fears we face, knowing that God's perspective is eternal, that nothing surprises our Savior, and that the Lord has a plan for every problem. To the Israelites facing a generation of exile and enslavement, the Lord whispered, "I know the plans I have for you. They are plans for good and not for disaster, to give you a future and a hope" (Jeremiah 29:11, NLT). Regardless of the fears that you're facing, you can conquer them by trusting in God's perspective and plan. Fear corrodes our confidence, but faith sees us through the storm. Furthermore, we can have faith in the presence of God.

PRESENCE

In *Green Lantern* the movie, Hal pilots an F-35 in a simulated dogfight against the prototype Sabre U-CAVs, flown by remote control. After leading the unmanned aircrafts above the service ceiling, Hal's jet stalls and careens earthward. Spiraling out of control and struggling to stay conscious, Hal fixes his eyes on a photo of his father and flashes back to his childhood. The young Hal asked his father, "You're not scared are you, Dad?" Resting a comforting hand on Hal's shoulder, Martin Jordan assured his son, "Let's just say it's my job not to be." Snapping back to the present, Hal regains his focus just in time to grab the pull handle and eject.[7]

Having his father's photo in the cockpit helped Hal to overcome his fear. Jesus does the same for us.

Do you know where Jesus was and what he was doing during this great tempest? The Bible says, "Jesus was in the stern, sleeping on a cushion" (Mark 4:38, NIV). The thunder clapped and the lightning struck, but Jesus slept soundly. Apparently, his disciples thought this meant that Jesus had fallen asleep at the wheel, so to speak. They wondered why he wasn't doing something. They focused so much on his apparent narcolepsy that they overlooked the most important fact: he was *there*. Jesus was with them in the boat. Asleep or awake, Immanuel—*God with us*—was present with them. The disciples looked around and saw danger. They looked within and saw fear. But they failed to look beside them and see Jesus.

In a similar instance, the disciples were caught in yet another fierce squall, and Jesus came to them walking on the water. As he approached his dread-filled disciples, he called out, "Don't be afraid! Take courage. I am here!" (Matthew 14:27, NLT). Just as Jesus accompanied his disciples in the boat, he's with us too. Wherever you may be, whatever dangers swirl around you, whatever fear swells up within you, Jesus is right beside you.

God is always with us. The Lord reminded Joshua, "Have I not commanded you? Be strong and courageous. Do not be afraid; do not be discouraged, for the LORD your God will be with you wherever you go" (Joshua 1:9, NIV). Before ascending into heaven, Jesus promised his followers, "And be sure of this: I am with you always, even to the end of the age" (Matthew 28:20, NLT). Jesus is always with you.

This promise reminds me of a story I once read. Five-year-old James was in the kitchen while his mom made supper. She asked him to go into the pantry and get her a can of tomato soup, but he didn't want to go alone. "It's dark in there, and I'm scared," he said. She asked again, but still James resisted. Finally she said, "It's okay, James. Jesus will be in there with you." So James walked hesitantly to the door and slowly opened it. He peeked inside, saw the darkness within, and his fears got the better of him. Not knowing what else to do, James called into the pantry, "Jesus, if you're in there, would you hand me a can of tomato soup?"

Jesus may not be physically in the pantry with you, but his Spirit lives in everyone who believes in him. Therefore, Jesus is with you wherever you go. He'll never leave you or forsake you. He could live anywhere in the universe, yet he chose your heart for his home. I don't know about you, but I would rather be in a storm with Jesus than anywhere else without him.

Just as a photo brought Hal Jordan into the reassuring presence of his father, remembrance of Christ's promise can usher us into God's presence. No matter what threats we face, real or imagined, the presence of God ought to calm our fears and strengthen our courage. Finally, just like the Green Lanterns, Christians can overcome great fear through faith in God's power.

POWER

Most Green Lanterns—including Hal Jordan, John Stewart, and Kyle Rayner—don't possess any inherent superpowers. But a Green Lantern's ring is regarded throughout the galaxy as the most powerful weapon in the universe, limited only by the bearer's imagination. It can conjure hard-light constructs of anything the wearer conceives. If a Green Lantern can imagine it, the ring can create it. In the movie, Jordan makes his debut as Green Lantern when a helicopter spirals out of control at a Ferris Aircraft gala. With the help of his ring, Hal quickly creates a life-size Hot Wheels car, complete with race track, to catch the careening copter before any harm can be done. With such great power literally at one's fingertips, it must be easy to overcome great fear.

But when it comes to conquering fear, Christians have an even greater power at our fingertips. When we feel afraid—when the struggles of this life overwhelm us, and it feels like our ship is about to sink—we can open our Bibles, listen to Jesus, and let the power of his Word calm the waves of fear raging within us.

When Christ's frightened followers cried out to him, the Bible says, "He awoke and rebuked the wind and said to the sea, 'Peace! Be still!' And the wind ceased, and there was a great calm" (Mark 4:39-40, ESV).

Can you imagine the awe and wonder that Jesus' followers felt at that moment? Jesus calmed the wind and the sea simply by the power of his word. Usually after the winds die down, the waves remain rough for hours, but in this case, everything became calm immediately and stayed that way. When God speaks, even the wind and the waves listen. Two thousand years later, the words of Jesus have not lost their power. God's Word is just as powerful as ever. Not only did the words of Jesus have the power to still the storm on the Sea of Galilee, but also, when you read his words splashed across the pages of your Bible, they have the power to still the storm within you.

Unlike a Green Lantern's ring, God's power isn't limited by our imagination. Rather, the Lord "is able to do immeasurably more than all we ask or imagine, according to his power that is at work within us" (Ephesians 3:20, NIV). The same God who was sovereign on the Sea of Galilee is sovereign over everything. And our Savior still calms the storms of life. Let the power of God work within you to settle your fears and fortify your faith.

✳✳✳

In the movie *Green Lantern*, Hal Jordan's longtime love interest, Carol Ferris, reminds him, "The ring didn't see that you were fearless. It saw that you had the ability to overcome fear."[8] The distinction is noteworthy. Hal Jordan and his fellow Lanterns weren't born without fear; rather, they learned to conquer fear. Likewise, we may never become fearless, but as we develop a stronger faith in God's perspective, presence, and power, we can learn to fear less.

NOTES
1. James Owsley (writer) and Mark Bright (artist), *Green Lantern: Emerald Dawn* #1 (DC Comics, 1989).

2. Geoff Johns (writer) and Ivan Reis (artist), *Green Lantern: Secret Origin* (DC Comics, 2008).

3. *Green Lantern*, directed by Martin Campbell (Warner Bros., 2011).

4. "Fear: What Americans Are Afraid of Today," *USA Weekend*, August 22–24, 1997, 5.

5. Charles Schulz, *Peanuts*, August 8, 1966 (available online: https://schulzmuseum.org/explore/press-room/peanuts-philosophies/).

6. Geoff Johns (writer) and Ivan Reis (artist), *Green Lantern: Secret Origin* (DC Comics, 2008).

7. *Green Lantern*, directed by Martin Campbell (Warner Bros., 2011).

8. Ibid.

7
STAR SAPPHIRE

I recently added yet another costume to my wife's already cramped costume closet: Green Lantern's longtime love interest, Carol Ferris, also known as Star Sapphire. Although I love the pairing of Hal and Carol, I hesitated to recreate the Star Sapphire costume, largely because it tends to be a bit too revealing. Like many comic book characters, Carol's costume has gone through many variations over the years. Whereas her first appearance featured her in a fairly modest long-sleeve pink leotard, more recent incarnations are often scantily clad. But my interest in creating a Star Sapphire costume recently renewed when watching *Green Lantern: The Animated Series* with my son. Not only does her costume appear more respectable, but also this retelling of her origin instantly piqued my interest.

While embattled against a space monster at the far reaches of the galaxy, Hal Jordan and his crew are rescued by a pair of violet-clad ring wielders known as the Star Sapphires. "So, you're what? Pink Lanterns?" Hal quips. "Not precisely, Green Lantern," the blue-skinned alien responds. "Where you value willpower, the Star Sapphires channel the power and serve the cause of love." Intrigued, Hal and his companions accompany the Star Sapphires to their home world, Zamaron. Their queen, Aga'po, tells Hal,

"My people believe that only love can save the universe." To which Princess Gi'ata quickly adds, "Love fuels our rings. Its power is unfathomable."

Eventually, with the help of his crew, Hal discovers that the Star Sapphires are not what they seem. Rather, these femme fatales use seduction and manipulation to win men's affections, and then they encase the men in sapphire, draining their victims of love. When Hal stands against them, Aga'po attempts to recruit Hal's one true love, Carol Ferris, teleporting her to Zamaron and offering her one of their sapphire rings. After a pitched battle of pink and green energy, Gi'ata tries to persuade Carol to control Hal, forcing him to stay with her rather than defend the galaxy as Green Lantern.

Carol responds, "Oh honey, that's not love. That's selfishness. Real love is sacrifice, putting another's needs before your own, doing what's best for the person you love." Hanging her head, Gi'ata admits, "You shame me, Carol Ferris. I did not truly understand love until now." In the aftermath of this revelation, Princess Gi'ata determines to teach her people the true meaning of love.[1]

This story offers a surprising parable about the scope and significance of love. Everybody loves love! We want to be loved, and we want to give love. It's the theme of a thousand songs, the topic of a million letters, and the subject of countless sermons. Our prayers, poems, and promises are all tethered to love. The problem is, our love is lacking. It's often conditional upon our own mood or our loved one's actions, appearance, or attitude. When it comes to love, all of us fall a little short, don't we?

Many of us face the same quandary as the Star Sapphires. We love the idea of love, but we lack a clear picture of what real love looks like. Later in the season, Carol returns to Zamaron to represent love in a battle between the Star Sapphires and the Red Lanterns, whose rings are fueled by hate. When asked about the true meaning of love, Carol hesitates. First she resorts to quoting song lyrics. But then she recalls another definition: "Love is patient. Love is kind…. It's not rude. It's not easily angered," she recites.[2]

The definition that Carol quotes is a biblical one, found in 1 Corinthians 13. Some of the most profound words ever scrawled about love are inscribed in this chapter of the Bible. No wonder Carol, and ultimately the rest of the Star Sapphires, find the words of this passage so transforming in developing a love worth wielding. The story of the Star Sapphires alongside 1 Corinthians 13 highlights three aspects of genuine love.

PROMINENCE OF LOVE

In the episode mentioned earlier, Hal and his crew discover that the Star Sapphires share a common ancestry with the Guardians of Oa. "Long ago, we were of one race with your masters," Queen Aga'po explains. "And usually hot girls don't go for the nerds," Hal jokes. "We took very different paths," Aga'po continues. "They refused to allow any emotion to influence their judgment. We found this insufferable and foolish." Queen Aga'po's final words as she and her followers left Oa forever were these: "Life without love is blasphemy."[3] For the Zamarons, love held the place of prominence in their hearts.

The same is true for the apostle Paul. In the prelude leading up to the Bible verses that Carol quoted, Paul wrote this: "If I could speak all the languages of earth and of angels, but didn't love others, I would only be a noisy gong or a clanging cymbal. If I had the gift of prophecy, and if I understood all of God's secret plans and possessed all knowledge, and if I had such faith that I could move mountains, but didn't love others, I would be nothing" (1 Corinthians 13:1-2, NLT).

In other words, without love, nothing else matters. A life without love is like a rainbow without colors or a sunset with no sun.

In the words of Queen Aga'po, "Life without love is blasphemy." I think that Jesus would have agreed.

Jesus was all about love. He commanded his followers to love one another, to love our neighbors, and even to love our enemies. In fact, when asked which of God's commands was the most important, Jesus answered, "'You must love the LORD your God with all your heart, all your soul, and all your mind.' This is the first and greatest commandment. A second is equally important: 'Love your neighbor as yourself.' The entire law and all the demands of the prophets are based on these two commandments" (Matthew 22:37-40, NLT). More than anything else, Jesus urged his listeners to love God and love people. He said that these two commands summarize all of Scripture. They pulse through the Bible like a heartbeat.

On the eve of his crucifixion, Jesus gathered his disciples together for one last meal and one last conversation. Over the course of the evening, as recorded in John 13–17, Jesus used the L-word no fewer than thirty-two times. Over and over he reiterates, "A new command I give you: Love one another. As I have loved you, so you must love one another. By this everyone will know that you are my disciples, if you love one another" (John 13:34-35, NIV).

It's clear that love was Jesus' highest priority. It should be ours too. My former pastor often said, "Life is all about who you love and who loves you in return." If you learn nothing else from this book, learn this: life is about love!

It doesn't matter how many degrees you earn or how many plaques decorate your wall if you don't love God. It doesn't matter how successful you are or how much money you make if you don't love your neighbor. It doesn't matter what you accomplish, accumulate, or achieve if you do it without love. Love is essential to a life well-lived. Make love your priority—but make sure what you prioritize is an accurate portrait of love.

PORTRAIT OF LOVE

Prior to Carol Ferris's intervention, the Star Sapphires devoted themselves to love. Love held their highest priority. Yet, they had a flawed understanding—a distorted picture—of love. After her encounter with Carol, Princess Gi'ata bursts into queen's quarters and announces, "Stop! We must release the men. We've been laboring under an imperfect understanding of love!"

They aren't the only ones. When I watch TV, browse the Internet, or scan magazines in the checkout lanes, it's clear to me that our world has an imperfect understanding of love. But in 1 Corinthians 13, the apostle Paul paints a beautiful portrait of real love. He writes, "Love is patient, love is kind. It does not envy, it does not boast, it is not proud. It does not dishonor others, it is not self-seeking, it is not easily angered, it keeps no record of wrongs. Love does not delight in evil but rejoices with the truth. It always protects, always trusts, always hopes, always perseveres" (1 Corinthians 13:4-7, NIV).

With a veritable kaleidoscope of phrases, Paul employs a full spectrum of ideas to offer a Technicolor portrait of love. In the original Greek, all fifteen of the terms that Paul utilizes are verbs. What this suggests is that love is not simply an intellectual abstraction or a passive notion; love is active. Love isn't just a fleeting feeling or a fickle emotion that flickers with the candlelight then vanishes. Love is love only when it acts. It's the conscious choice to be polite (because love is not rude), generous (because love is not self-seeking), slow to anger (because love is not easily angered), and quick to forgive (because love keeps no record of wrongs). This is what real love looks like.

Unfortunately, as we leap from verb to verb, we discover a standard that none of us live up to. Carol recognized her own limitations when the Star Sapphires turned to her for answers about love. She explained, "Love is about doing what's best for the one you love. It's as simple as putting his or her needs above your own. But I'm no expert." In truth, none of us are.

When performing weddings, I've often challenged the couple to replace the word *love* in this passage with their own names. Have you ever tried that? I have: "Scott is patient. Scott is kind. He does not envy, he does not boast, he is not proud." Sadly, I can't make it through all four verses without lying about myself. I'll bet you can't either.

This passage paints a portrait of love that none of us can match. None, that is, except Jesus. Plug his name into these verses, and every word still rings true. Jesus is patient. Jesus is kind. Jesus doesn't envy, he doesn't boast, he's not proud. Jesus is not rude, or self-seeking, or easily angered. Jesus keeps no record of wrongs. Jesus doesn't delight in evil but rejoices with the truth. Jesus always protects, always trusts, always hopes, always perseveres.

Jesus is the only one of us who resembles the portrait that Paul paints. That's why Jesus urges us, "I have loved you even as the Father has loved me. Live within my love" (John 15:9, TLB). Here Jesus reveals the secret to loving God and others: living loved. Receive the love of Jesus. Live in his love. Let the love of God saturate your heart. His love can fill your heart and spill into every part of your life. Imagine that. Imagine living your life with his heart. Wouldn't you be more patient with your family? Less envious of the neighbors? Less boastful at work? Focus your mind's eye until you have a clear picture of the heart of Jesus leading your life. Now snap the shutter and frame the picture. This is what real love looks like.

PERMANENCE OF LOVE

In the episode in which Carol quoted Scripture, she returned to Zamaron at the command of Aya, an artificial intelligence with a broken heart. Aya began as a navigation system aboard Hal

Jordan's spaceship, the *Interceptor*. Working alongside Hal and his crew, Aya developed a yearning to be more than a machine. She longed to become a Green Lantern herself. So, using spare parts from the ship, she assembled her own android body and became part of the team. During their mission in Frontier Space, Aya even fell in love with another member of the crew, a Red Lantern named Razor. At first, Razor reciprocates Aya's feelings, confessing his love. But later, he denies his affection. "I do not love you. At all. I cannot," Razor coldly explains. "You are just a machine, and I can never love you." As Razor walks away, Aya is left sullen and speechless. "Processing…processing…processing…"—the word continues to fall from her lips like a computer program stuck in a loop.

Overcome by heartache, Aya chooses to shut off all emotions and wrests control of a powerful being called the Anti-Monitor. Now a cold emotionless entity, Aya sets out to destroy Zamaron, accusing them, "I have gained the understanding that the emotion you serve—love—is not only useless, but destructive. I loved and was loved, only to have that love retracted…leaving me nothing but pain."[4]

In Aya's positronic mind, love failed her. Maybe you've felt the same way. Maybe those who should have loved you didn't. Maybe those who could have loved you didn't. Maybe your love tank has been running low lately. Maybe you haven't felt very loved, or maybe you feel like you don't have any more love to give. Don't give up.

Others may promise and fail, but God's love never fails. "Love never stops being patient, never stops believing, never stops hoping, never gives up. Love never comes to an end" (1 Corinthians 13:7-8, GW). Real love doesn't give up when life gets tough. Real love doesn't walk away just because it's easier. It perseveres through all the trials and troubles of life. Another translation sums it up this way: "Love never fails."

The Bible says, "We know how much God loves us because we have felt his love and because we believe him when he tells us that he loves us dearly. God is love, and anyone who lives in love is living with God and God is living in him" (1 John 4:16, TLB). God loves you with an unconditional, unrelenting, unfailing love. God's love never stops, never runs out, never gives up. God's love never comes to an end.

***

Queen Aga'po was right when she told Hal Jordan, "Only love can save the universe." And thanks to Carol Ferris's recollection of a biblical definition of love, the Star Sapphires learned the true significance and scope of love. Paul concludes his thesis on love with these words: "Three things will last forever—faith, hope, and love—and the greatest of these is love" (1 Corinthians 13:13, NLT). If you need to experience the kind of love that Paul describes, I urge you to open your heart to the love of God. His love—if you'll let it—can fill your heart and change your life.

NOTES

1. "In Love and War," *Green Lantern: The Animated Series* #9 (Cartoon Network, 2012).

2. "Love Is a Battlefield," *Green Lantern: The Animated Series* #22 (Cartoon Network, 2013).

3. Peter Tomasi (writer) and Patrick Gleason (artist), *Green Lantern Corps* #29 (DC Comics, 2008).

4. "Love Is a Battlefield," *Green Lantern: The Animated Series* #22 (Cartoon Network, 2013).

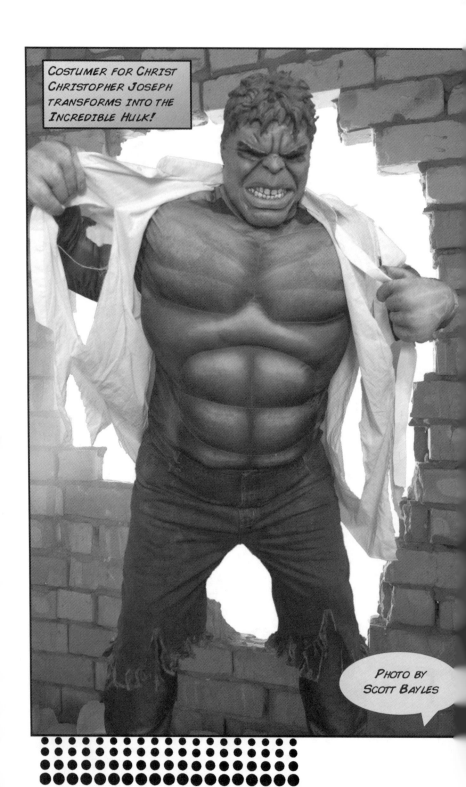

8
HULK

If there is one comic book character that I may never cosplay as, it's the Hulk. Okay, I'll never be Wonder Woman either, but for completely different reasons. It's not that I don't want to be the Hulk. The Incredible Hulk is easily one of the most iconic and beloved characters in comics history. He's also one of the hardest to cosplay.

I've seen few worthwhile attempts at reproducing the Hulk's heroic proportions. Some fitness fanatics with their own bulging biceps simply air-brush their bodies green, reminiscent of Lou Ferrigno's famous portrayal in the 1970s television show. But with three kids and a full-time ministry, I don't see myself spending the two to three hours per day in the gym necessary to build up a hulking physique. Others try tackling the green giant by crafting elaborate muscle padding made of foam and latex. These rarely look believable and are awkward and uncomfortable to wear. No doubt that's why Marvel went the route of computer-generated imagery in the last few movies featuring Hulk. But, despite my diminishing hope of ever cosplaying as the Hulk, I still find his story compelling.

After designing and overseeing the construction of a gamma bomb, Dr. Bruce Banner organized the first test detonation in the

New Mexico desert. But in an unforeseeable accident, Banner himself was caught in the blast and bombarded with gamma radiation. Now Bruce finds himself transformed—physically and psychologically—in times of anger and outrage, becoming seven feet tall and one thousand pounds of uncontrolled fury—"the most powerful creature to ever walk the earth," says Stan Lee.[1]

In *Ultimate Avengers: The Movie*, Nick Fury describes the Hulk to Captain America, saying, "There's a monster inside the good doctor. Every time he finds himself even a little upset that beast comes out. The madder he gets, the stronger he gets, and the more landscape he levels. He becomes raw, unleashed rage—a hulking monster right out of your worst nightmares."[2] Hunted by the military and haunted by the monster lurking within him, Bruce Banner travels the world in search of a cure. Hulk's problems are encapsulated in actor Bill Bixby's famous line from *The Incredible Hulk* television series: "Don't make me angry. You wouldn't like me when I'm angry."[3]

Stan Lee's tale of a man's unbridled anger transforming him into a giant, green rage-monster strikes a chord with countless fans. After all, Dr. Banner isn't the first person to struggle with anger. There's a monster lurking within each one of us. When our hearts fill with fury, we hurt the people we love. We say things that we know we shouldn't say and then wonder why we said them. We can be downright beastly, you and I.

Unsurprisingly, the Bible has much to say about anger. In fact, as we peruse the pages of Scripture we find at least three different types of anger that the Hulk himself experiences, as well as guidance on how to handle each one.

SUDDEN ANGER

The first and most common form of anger is sudden outbursts of anger. Black Widow was once on the receiving end of Hulk's sudden anger. In Marvel's *The Avengers*, an explosion on the Helicarrier isolates Dr. Banner and Black Widow. Pinned down by debris, Black Widow helplessly watches as Bruce violently morphs into the Hulk. As rage takes over, the Hulk lashes out without restraint. Freeing her injured leg, Widow tries to escape as the Hulk smashes his way through the bowels of the ship. But the Hulk is too fast and too furious to elude. Hulk backhands Black Widow, launching her into the air. Thor comes to the rescue before Hulk can do any further damage, but Black Widow is nonetheless left cringing in the corner, hugging her knees and trembling with fear.[4]

The Bible says, "An angry person starts fights; a hot-tempered person commits all kinds of sin" (Proverbs 29:22, NLT). It also says, "Short-tempered people do foolish things" (Proverbs 14:17, NLT). We already knew that, of course, because we experience it first-hand. We may blame our hot temper on our hair color or heritage, but the bottom line is this: if we have a short fuse, we do a lot of foolish things. You may not transform into a giant green rage-monster, but you might turn red in the face, throw a temper tantrum, or experience road rage. How many times have you said something in anger that you wished you could take back the moment the words left your lips? As Will Rogers once said, "Whenever you fly into a rage, you seldom make a safe landing." Sadly, as was the case with Hulk and Black Widow, it's often the people closest to us whom we end up hurting the most when we lose control.

So how do we handle sudden anger? The Bible says, "People with quick tempers cause trouble, but those who control their tempers stop a quarrel" (Proverbs 15:18, NCV). And again, "Foolish people lose their tempers, but wise people control theirs" (Proverbs 29:11, NCV). Control is the key. While it may be easier said than done, there are a variety of ways to control your temper.

In Marvel's 2008 movie *The Incredible Hulk*, knowing how destructive the Hulk can be, Dr. Banner works to develop multiple techniques for controlling his anger. He practices meditation and breathing techniques in order to calm himself down in stressful situations. He also wears a heart-rate monitor that alerts him whenever his pulse rises too high. In a humorous scene following a harrowing cab ride through New York, Betty Ross flips out at the cab driver, screaming, "Are you out of our mind? What is wrong with you?" To which Bruce calmly responds, "You know, I know a few techniques that could help you manage that anger effectively."[5]

We could benefit from those techniques too. While a digital pulse indicator may not be necessary, all of us ought to monitor our tempers. First, you can be aware of what sets you off and avoid those things the best you can. Furthermore, you can pay close attention to how your body experiences stress. You won't turn green and hulk-out, but perhaps your muscles tighten, your breath quickens, or your stomach churns. These can be early warning signs of a rising temper. Finally, prayer and meditating on God's Word can also help control our tempers. If you've accepted Jesus as your Heavenly Hero, then you have the added assistance of his Holy Spirit. The Bible says one of the fruit of the Spirit is "self-control" (Galatians 5:22-23). When you feel yourself starting to lose your temper, you can quickly go to God in prayer and ask him to fill your heart with his Spirit. The very act of breathing a prayer may be enough to extinguish a flare-up of sudden anger.

However, frequent bouts of sudden anger can often point to a deeper problem: stubborn anger.

STUBBORN ANGER

Dr. Banner struggles with this second type of anger as well. In the final battle scene of Marvel's *The Avengers*, Captain America turns to Bruce as an alien horde invades New York and announces, "Doctor Banner, I think now might be a good time for you to get angry." Bruce replies, "That's my secret, Cap. I'm *always* angry."[6] Always angry, huh?

Maybe you can relate to the good doctor. Do you wake up mad? Go to sleep bitter? Do hostility and resentment catapult to the surface when someone triggers your emotions? If you answered yes to any of those questions, you may be saddled with stubborn anger.

Stubborn anger is the type of anger that lingers and festers day after day. You walk around with a chip on your shoulder and a grudge against the world. Stubborn, or chronic, anger doesn't just happen overnight. In many cases, sudden anger issues, left uncontrolled, gradually build over a period of years. Other times, traumatic events can lead to festering feeling of rage. In *The Incredible Hulk* television series, starring Bill Bixby and Lou Ferrigno, Dr. Banner wrestles with overwhelming grief over the death of his wife, Laura.[7] This unresolved grief mutates into pent-up anger over time. In Ang Lee's 2003 retelling, *Hulk*, Bruce's struggle with stubborn anger results from childhood abuse at the hands of his father.[8] Of course, these persistent feelings of anger make Hulk (and us) more prone to eruptions of sudden anger.

The Bible, of course, has something to say about this type of anger too: "Don't let the sun go down while you are still angry, for anger gives a foothold to the devil" (Ephesians 4:26-27, NLT). In other words, when we let our anger go unresolved, we give the devil a place to work in our hearts and relationships. The Bible then urges us, "Get rid of all bitterness, rage, anger, harsh words, and slander, as well as all types of evil behavior. Instead, be kind to each other, tenderhearted, forgiving one another, just as God through Christ has forgiven you" (Ephesians 4:31-32, NLT).

Stubborn anger needs to be conquered. And the key to conquering stubborn anger is forgiveness.

In Marvel's latest animated incarnation, *Hulk and the Agents of S.M.A.S.H.*, the Hulk teams up with his old enemy General "Thunderbolt" Ross to take down another gamma-powered monster known as Abomination. Ross not only spent years hunting the Hulk, but he also created Abomination in an ill-conceived gamma experiment. In a poignant exchange, Abomination questions Hulk, "How can you be friends with a man who spent years trying to destroy you?" Without a moment's hesitation, Hulk responds, "Simple. I forgave him." Abomination's eye widen with disbelief, as he chides, "You're a bigger fool than I thought." Hulk's response speaks to all of us: "Only a fool holds on to a bad past. If I can forgive him, you can too."[9]

Your bitterness may be due to an abusive parent, a hypercritical spouse, ungrateful children, an overly demanding boss, a venomous ex-spouse, a judgmental pastor, or a friend's betrayal. But the solution in each case is forgiveness: "Forgive one another, just as God through Christ has forgiven you." Forgiveness isn't always easy, but by holding onto our hurts, bearing a grudge, or harboring resentment, we only hurt ourselves. This is why Jesus taught his disciples to pray, "Forgive us our sins, as we have forgiven those who sin against us" (Matthew 6:12, NLT). Only forgiveness has the power to conquer deep-seated, stubborn anger.

SANCTIFIED ANGER

Fortunately, not all anger is sinful. "Be angry and do not sin," the Bible urges (Ephesians 4:26, ESV). The ancient Greek philosopher Aristotle put it this way: "Anyone can become angry—that is easy. But to become angry with the right person, to the right degree, at the right time, for the right purpose, and in the right way—that is not easy." This is precisely what sanctified anger is: righteous anger channeled in the right direction.

When the Hulk channels his anger in the right direction, he becomes an unstoppable force for good. He has single-handedly defeated brutish beasts like Abomination, would-be world conquerors like Leader, and even entire armadas of alien invaders like the Skrull. In *Hulk and the Agents of S.M.A.S.H.*, Big Green is no longer a mindless aberration. Rather, Hulk regulates his rage as he leads a whole team of gamma-charged cohorts including She-Hulk, Red Hulk (General Ross), A-Bomb, and Skaar. In the first episode, a doorway to the extradimensional Negative Zone mysteriously opens in Hulk's hometown of Vista Verde. In a battle that rages across realms, Hulk and his colorful companions turn back a full-scale alien invasion lead by Annihilus, Lord of the Negative Zone—an amazing display of productive anger.[10]

If you will learn to control and channel your anger as well as the Hulk, you can do tremendous things. The Bible portrays God as the angriest of all. Of the 455 uses of the word *anger* in the Old Testament, 375 of them refer to God's anger. And in the New Testament, Jesus also demonstrates righteous or sanctified anger. The Savior who tenderly held little children in his arms also violently overturned tables in the temple. If you can become as good at expressing your anger as was God or Jesus, you will be able to channel the power of anger toward great ends.

I'm reminded again of Captain America's remark: "Doctor Banner, I think now might be a good time for you to get angry." Now might be a good time for Christians to get angry. Sometimes an infusion of sanctified anger may be the very thing the church needs. Anger at injustice in various forms. Anger at abuse. Anger at bullying. Anger at rape. Anger at persecution and prejudice. Anger at human trafficking. Anger at world hunger and children in poverty. Anger at hypocrisy and hardheartedness. Anger at the sin within our own hearts. If we would get angry about the right things, to the right intensity, at the right time, for the right purpose, and channel that anger in the right direction, we could do great good. We could feed the hungry, shelter the homeless, help the hurting, strengthen families, share the gospel, and experience life-changing spiritual transformation on a hulking scale. If you've learned to harness the power of sanctified anger and channel it in a constructive way, then now might be a good time for you to get angry.

HOLY HEROES

***

The Hulk demonstrates all kinds of anger—both good and bad. So be angry, but don't sin. Don't let the sun go down on your wrath. Don't allow the devil to have a foothold in your life. If you are consistently struggling with sinful outbursts of sudden anger or unresolved stubborn anger, you may want to talk with a trusted pastor or Christian counselor who can help you control, conquer, and channel your anger. Who knows? Maybe then people might actually like you when you're angry!

NOTES

1. Stan Lee (writer) and Jack Kirby (artist), *Incredible Hulk* #1 (Marvel Comics, 1962).

2. *Ultimate Avengers: The Movie*, directed by Curt Geda and Steven E. Gordon (Lions Gate Films, 2006).

3. *The Incredible Hulk* (CBS Television, 1978–1982).

4. *Marvel's The Avengers*, directed by Joss Whedon (Walt Disney Studios, 2012).

5. *The Incredible Hulk*, directed by Louis Leterrier (Universal Studios, 2008).

6. *Marvel's The Avengers*, directed by Joss Whedon (Walt Disney Studios, 2012).

7. *The Incredible Hulk* (CBS Television, 1978–1982).

8. *Hulk*, directed by Ang Lee (Universal Pictures, 2003).

9. "Abomination," *Hulk and the Agents of S.M.A.S.H.* #17 (Disney XD, 2014).

10. "Doorway to Destruction," *Hulk and the Agents of S.M.A.S.H.* #1 (Disney XD, 2013).

9
SPIDER-MAN

In 2013, while our family was volunteering as the Avengers for the Route 66 Mother Road Festival in Springfield, Illinois, I learned of a little boy named Tyler. Radiation treatments kept Tyler's lymphoma at bay, but they also kept him from the festival that day. I told Tyler's mom about Costumers for Christ, and she told me that Tyler would absolutely love a visit from his favorite superhero, Spider-Man.

Although I made several Spider-Man costumes as commissioned works, this was the first time I cosplayed as Spider-Man. Saint John's Children's Hospital was colorful and inviting. Both patients and staff smiled brightly as Spidey walked the halls and rode the elevator to the fifth floor. A somewhat startled security guard pointed me to Tyler's room. But when I poked my head through his door, what I saw surprised me. I expected a frail little boy too weak to move. But as soon as Tyler saw Spider-Man, he jumped out of bed and ran over to meet me, energetically bounding around the room. He spewed forth enough Spider-Man knowledge to impress any fan. As we talked, I learned that Tyler is in "maintenance" now, which means he still has radiation treatments on a regular basis, but has been cancer-free for several months. Praise God!

A bright little boy, it didn't take Tyler long to notice that I wasn't hanging upside down from the ceiling or sticking to the walls. "You're not the real Spider-Man, are you?"

I smiled behind my mask and confessed, "You're right, Tyler. I'm not really Spider-Man. That's because superheroes like Superman, Batman, and Spider-Man are just pretend. But there is one real Superhero who came to earth a long time ago with special powers and abilities. He even gave his life to save the world." Then I asked, "Would you like to read a comic book about that hero?" Tyler nodded expectantly, and I handed him a copy of *The Amazing Gospel*.

Surprisingly, Tyler wasn't the least bit disappointed to find out that I wasn't the real Spider-Man. Instead, he said that he loved my costume, told me all about his own Spidey costume, and asked to try on my mask. Before saying goodbye, I reminded Tyler of the sage advice that Uncle Ben once gave to Peter Parker: "With great power comes great responsibility."

Those words are the heartbeat of Spider-Man comics, cartoons, and cinema.

Let me give some background for those who are unfamiliar with the story. The spectacular Spider-Man started off as puny Peter Parker, a brainy and bookish teenager at Mid-Town High in New York. But one day, while attending a science exhibit, Peter was bitten by a radioactive spider and imbued with the proportionate strength and agility of an arachnid. Suddenly Peter could scale walls and ceilings, and he developed a precognitive "spider-sense" that warns him of impending danger.

Peter first used his newfound powers selfishly, to earn money and fame. In a pivotal moment, Peter witnessed a robbery, but rather than help catch the crook, Peter just looked the other way—a decision that would haunt him for the rest of his life. That night, Peter's Uncle Ben died after being shot by the very same thief that Peter allowed to escape.

This is the defining moment in Spider-Man's origin story. In his grief, Peter finally realized what his surrogate father, Uncle Ben, had been trying so hard to teach him: with great power comes great responsibility. This maxim becomes the moral compass that guides Spider-Man's heroic adventures.

Long before Stan Lee scripted the story of Spider-Man, though, the Bible said something very similar: "When someone has been given much, much will be required in return; and when someone has been entrusted with much, even more will be required" (Luke 12:48, NLT). Peter had tremendous power entrusted to him, but in a life-altering choice, he declined to take responsibility for intervening in the face of wrongdoing.

In some interesting ways, Spider-Man's origin story has striking similarities to a story that Jesus told: the parable of the good Samaritan. It's as well-known as the story of Spidey himself—and maybe more so!

Jesus' parable is a timeless tale about a man walking down a dangerous road in a perilous part of town. He falls victim to robbers on his journey, and as was the case with Peter Parker, others passed by the scene and chose not to get involved. Here's how Jesus tells it:

> As a man was going down from Jerusalem to Jericho, some robbers attacked him. They tore off his clothes, beat him, and left him lying there, almost dead. It happened that a priest was going down that road. When he saw the man, he walked by on the other side. Next, a Levite came there, and after he went over and looked at the man, he walked by on the other side of the road. Then a Samaritan traveling down the road came to where the hurt man was. When he saw the man, he felt very sorry for him. The Samaritan went to him, poured olive oil and wine on his wounds, and bandaged them.

Then he put the hurt man on his own donkey and took him to an inn where he cared for him. The next day, the Samaritan brought out two coins, gave them to the innkeeper, and said, "Take care of this man. If you spend more money on him, I will pay it back to you when I come again." (Luke 10:30-35, NCV)

Keep this biblical story in mind as we examine the story of Spider-Man. Within each story we encounter familiar character types traveling the same road but with very different attitudes in their hearts.

CRUEL HEARTS

In the graphic novel *Ultimate Spider-Man: Power and Responsibility*, a grief-stricken Aunt May sits in her living room surrounded by police officers and her distraught nephew, Peter, as she recounts the evening's tragic events. "We—we heard a noise in the back," she recalls. "And right then—I don't know why—but right then I knew something was wrong. I knew that someone was in our house." Tears cascade over her cheeks as she continues, "He—he was standing there in the doorway—he was shaking—and he asked us where we kept our money. Ben told him we didn't have any. And we don't. Nothing."

In the next panel Aunt May's eyes fill with horror at the memory. "And the guy just got real agitated and screamed: 'Give me all your money!' And Ben—he—he just, he…." May's heart sinks as she stares at the chalk outline marking the Parkers' bloodstained floor. "And that was that. He just ran out the way he came."[1]

Uncle Ben's killer, like the attackers in Jesus' tale, was nameless, and he was cruel. He simply appeared, threatened Ben and May, then shot Ben and left him for dead. Sadly, stories of criminal cruelty such as these aren't relegated to comic books or the canon of Scripture.

The real world is full of villains. You can hardly turn on the news without seeing the stories. Parents leave a special-needs child locked in a cage until she dies of starvation. A sixteen-year-old beats to death an eighty-five-year-old with no apparent motive. Gang violence takes innocent victims in the crossfire. Gunmen slaughter kindergarteners. Terrorists crash planes. Our world is all too familiar with criminals and killers. In one of the darkest corners of the New Testament, the apostle Paul pulls together the Old Testament's bleak assessments of humanity:

> As the Scriptures say:…"There is no one who does anything good; there is not even one." "Their throats are like open graves; they use their tongues for telling lies." "Their words are like snake poison." "Their mouths are full of cursing and hate." "They are always ready to kill people. Everywhere they go they cause ruin and misery. They don't know how to live in peace." "They have no fear of God." (Romans 3:10-18, NCV)

Sadly, this biblical passage isn't talking about the Philistines, the Canaanites, or even garden-variety pagans. It describes humanity in general. Ever since Cain killed Abel, human hands have shed innocent blood. The robbers in Jesus' parable, and the robber who murdered Peter's Uncle Ben, are a reminder of how dark and disturbing our world can be.

Of course, not every heart is so cold and cruel; some hearts are simply calloused.

CALLOUSED HEARTS

It's been well said, "All that is necessary for the triumph of evil is that good men do nothing." That's just what Peter Parker did. Nothing. And because of Peter's inaction, evil triumphed in Aunt May's living room.

In Sam Raimi's retelling of Spidey's origin in the 2002 film, Peter stands with a goofy grin stretched across his face in the office of a disreputable wrestling promoter. As Peter anxiously waits to collect his winnings, the agent slides a $100 bill across his desk. "A hundred bucks? The ad said three thousand," Peter complains. "Well, check it again web-head," the shady publicist replies. "It said three grand for three minutes. You pinned him in two. For that I give you a hundred. And you're lucky to get that." Peter protests, "I need that money." To which the crooked promoter wisecracks, "I missed the part where that's my problem."

Moments later a gun-wielding thief bursts in demanding money. As the criminal makes his escape, he runs right past Peter, who simply steps aside. The publicist whines to Peter, "You could have taken that guy apart! Now he's gonna get away with my money." Peter just smirks and says, "I missed the part where that's my problem."[2]

"Not my problem." Those very words could easily have fallen from the lips of the bystanders who appear in Jesus' parable. As an innocent victim lies dying on the side of the road, he is ignored not once, but twice, by people who could have helped; they just "passed him by" (Luke 10:31-32).

Did you notice that these two passersby were not your average temple-goers? These were the religious leaders of Jerusalem—a priest and a Levite ("temple assistant" [NLT]). Neither of these men was violent or abusive, like the robbers, yet when they saw someone in need of help, they did nothing. Even though they had the power to help, they didn't see it as their responsibility. Their hearts were calloused.

Sadly, like those religious leaders and like the young Peter Parker, many of us share their mentality.

As a culture, we desensitize ourselves to the needs around us. The world is full of hurting people. I shudder to consider how many of them we have passed by on the other side. Nearly two billion people are desperately poor,[3] one billion are hungry,[4] millions are trafficked in slavery, and twenty-one thousand children die every day from preventable diseases.[5] Earthquakes, tsunamis, and tornadoes devastate neighborhoods and nations. We see commercials about starving children in the Horn of Africa and instinctively change the channel. We see the hungry and homeless holding signs on street corners, only to avoid eye contact until the light turns green. "Not my problem," we tell ourselves. "They don't deserve my help," we rationalize. "It's not my responsibility," we insist. It's just easier to do nothing.

But that is how evil triumphs. John F. Kennedy, aptly alluding to Dante's *Inferno*, once said, "The hottest places in hell are reserved for those who, during a time of great moral crisis, do nothing." Because Peter did nothing, his Uncle Ben was killed. Because the priest and the Levite did nothing, an innocent man almost died. Thankfully, neither of these stories ends here. The final heart-condition that we see in these parables is a compassionate heart—that of the Samaritan and, as we will see, that of Peter Parker.

COMPASSIONATE HEARTS

Peter learned a painful but life-changing lesson when he lost his uncle. In *Ultimate Spider-Man* #7, Peter reflects on his uncle's last words to him: "Great things are going to happen to you in your life, Peter. Great things. And with that will come great responsibility. Do you understand?" Then Peter whispers, "I do now…. You were right—with power comes responsibility. Absolutely. For some reason I've been given great power. And with great power then must come great responsibility. I will never let you down again, Uncle Ben."[6] From that moment on, Peter dedicated his life to helping those in need as their friendly, neighborhood Spider-Man. His callous heart had been transformed by grief into a heart of compassion.

In Jesus' parable, we don't see such a transformation, but we do see a remarkable contrast. While the religious leaders in the story were callous toward the wounded victim, another character appears on the barren boulevard. Just as the sun began to set over the horizon, perhaps, a Samaritan man comes around the bend.

For the original audience of this parable, the Samaritan's appearance would have struck a foreboding note. Although Jews and Samaritans were separate branches of the same family tree, they had become enemies. In fact, a woman once reminded Jesus, "Jews refuse to have anything to do with Samaritans" (John 4:9, NLT). The Jews of Jesus' day discriminated against and looked down upon the Samaritans.

Jesus' listeners would have expected the Samaritan to turn a blind eye, just as the Jewish leaders had done. Instead, Jesus said that when the newcomer saw the dying man, "He felt compassion for him" (Luke 10:33, NLT). First, the Samaritan tended the man's wounds. Then, he provided transportation to the nearest ancient Best Western. Finally, going the extra mile, he paid the bill and promised to cover any additional expenses.

Today, the expression "good Samaritan" is synonymous with good deeds and helping others. In fact, the dictionary defines it as "one who is compassionate and helpful to a person in distress." The volunteer workers at Saint John's Children's Hospital, where I visited Tyler, are even called Samaritans. All this is because Jesus made a Samaritan the unexpected hero of his story.

***

While Superman reminds us that we have a hero in Jesus, Spider-Man reminds us that we can be a hero to those in need. You don't have to spin webs, stick to walls, or have the proportionate strength of a spider to be someone's hero. All you need is a caring and compassionate heart.

Hopefully, it doesn't take the loss of a loved one for us to follow in Peter Parker's footsteps. When you see suffering or injustice, please don't just look the other way. Don't withhold good from those in need when it's in your power to help them. The Bible says, "See that no one pays back evil for evil, but always try to do good to each other and to all people" (1 Thessalonians 5:15, NLT). Let this command be the moral compass on whatever road you travel, and, in so doing, become the hero in someone's story—the hero God made you to be.

NOTES

1. Brian Michael Bendis (writer) and Mark Bagley (artist), "Power and Responsibility," *Ultimate Spider-Man* #1 (Marvel Comics, 2001).

2. *Spider-Man*, directed by Sam Raimi (Columbia Pictures, 2002).

3. DoSomething.org, "11 Facts About Global Poverty," https://www.dosomething.org/facts/11-facts-about-global-poverty.

4. Martin Penner, "Number Of World's Hungry Tops A Billion," June 19, 2009, WFP.org, http://www.wfp.org/stories/number-world-hungry-tops-billion.

5. Anup Shah, "Today, Around 21,000 Children Died Around the World," Global Issues.org, September 24, 2011, http://www.globalissues.org/article/715/today-21000-children-died-around-the-world.

6. Brian Michael Bendis (writer) and Mark Bagley (artist), "Irresponsible," *Ultimate Spider-Man* #7 (Marvel Comics, 2006).

THE BAYLES FAMILY COSPLAYS SOME OF THE CLASSIC X-MEN, INCLUDING CYCLOPS, JEAN GREY AND NIGHT CRAWLER!

EFFECTS BY DEREK RAYNER OF TORCHBEARER GRAPHICS!

PHOTO BY FRIENDLY BYSTANDER

10
X-MEN

I first discovered Marvel's X-Men at age twelve. I spent countless hours watching the animated exploits of Cyclops, Wolverine, Storm, Beast, Rogue, and Jubilee as part of the Fox Kids Saturday morning lineup. I delighted in the bright yellow and blue costumes and the swashbuckling adventure. Most kids my age revered Wolverine, but I favored Cyclops. Cyclops led the team, and, like me, he was a tall redhead whose real name was Scott. How could I not like him? I held many fond memories of that cartoon series, so when we first cosplayed as the X-Men in 2010, I based our costume designs on those versions of the characters. Naturally, I was Cyclops. Ashley portrayed Cyclops's romantic counterpart, Jean Grey. Our son played Wolverine, and our girls dressed as Rogue and Shadowcat.

A couple of years later, I revamped our costumes to reflect the original founding members of the X-Men. Commonly called the First Class, the original team of five included Cyclops and Jean Grey (then called Marvel Girl), along with Beast, Angel, and Iceman. This first class of X-Men date back to 1963, when Stan Lee co-created them along with artist Jack Kirby. Teenagers all over the country identified with the eclectic characters, and the X-Men enjoyed tremendous success all through the 1970s, becoming the most collected team book in comics. Since then, the X-Men have featured in several cartoon series, a steady flow of video games, and seven feature films.

When Stan Lee first came up with the concept for the X-Men, he admitted in an interview that his biggest struggle was figuring out how they all got their super powers. He said, "I couldn't have everybody bitten by radioactive spiders or hit by gamma rays…so I took the lazy way out."[1] Rather than acquiring their powers in some freak accident like other superheroes, the X-Men were simply born with their powers due to a genetic mutation. At Xavier's School for Gifted Youngsters, a powerful telepath named Charles Xavier provides guidance and direction for the young mutants. Lovingly referred to by his students as Professor X, the wheelchair-bound mentor trains his pupils to use their powers for the benefit of humanity.

The story of the X-Men actually shares much in common with the story of God's chosen people. Without getting too deep into the X-Men's rich history and character backgrounds, I want to highlight three similarities between the tale of the X-Men and the truth of Christ-followers today.

A PECULIAR PEOPLE

In the comics, mutants differ from ordinary people. They possess special powers and abilities that come from an "X-gene," a genetic abnormality that causes random mutations. Most of the X-Men still look like ordinary people, but those who don't often do their best to hide their differences. In Marvel's movie *X-Men: First Class*, a mutant named Mystic possesses blue skin and the ability to shape-shift at will, but she uses her shape-changing ability to look normal at all times, being afraid of what people might think.[2] In the third X-Men movie, *Last Stand*, Warren Worthington—also known as Angel—wears an uncomfortable harness to hide his enormous wings.[3] But no matter how the mutants appear on the surface, this X-gene along with their special abilities sets them apart from the rest of the world. They're outsiders who never really fit in. They're uncanny. They're peculiar. And so are Christians.

In fact, the King James Version of the Bible actually uses that very word in describing God's chosen people: "But ye are a chosen generation, a royal priesthood, an holy nation, a peculiar people" (1 Peter 2:9, KJV). Normally when we see the word *peculiar*, it is referring to someone or something that is strange, odd, or uncommon. But it can be used to describe something or someone that "belongs exclusively to some person, group, or thing" or to "a property or privilege belonging exclusively or characteristically to a person."[4] In other words, Scripture is saying that Christians are different from other people. They have characteristics that identify them as belonging exclusively to God. The God's Word Translation puts it this way: "you are chosen people...people who belong to God" (1 Peter 2:9, GW).

I remember getting some strange looks in high school when my friends found out I attended church with my family not once a week, but three times a week. People may find you peculiar for praying before your meals, choosing church attendance over sleeping late on Sunday, or living your life according to different values. And while those things do make us superficially different, what truly makes Christians peculiar is that, as believers in Jesus Christ, we are the personal possession of God.

Just as mutants are born with an X-gene inside of them, believers are born again when Jesus places his Spirit within us, marking us as his own. Rather than being "children of the atom," as the X-Men are often called, we are the children of God. We're not like other people in the world. We're more than different: we're unique. And so, we live unique lives to the glory of God.

Unfortunately, being different often results in being misunderstood, and even mistreated. The second similarity between X-Men and Christians is that both are a persecuted people.

A PERSECUTED PEOPLE

A dominant theme in the X-Men comics and movies is a growing fear and hatred of mutants by the rest of the world. A recurring X-Men antagonist in comics, cartoons, and movies is Robert Kelly, a prominent U.S. senator who built his career on an anti-mutant platform. He often argues that mutants are a danger to "normal" people and should be forced to register with the government.

The comics and cartoons often feature stories of mutants being mistreated or even hunted down and locked away. Long-time X-Men writer Chris Claremont said, "The X-Men are hated, feared, and despised collectively by humanity for no other reason than that they are mutants. So what we have,...intended or not, is a book that is about racism, bigotry, and prejudice."[5]

While there are obvious social and political undertones to the X-Men's plight, their persecution is something that, historically and globally, Christians can identify with very well. Jesus told his disciples, "If the world hates you, remember that it hated me first. The world would love you as one of its own if you belonged to it, but you are no longer part of the world. I chose you to come out of the world, so it hates you.... Since they persecuted me, naturally they will persecute you" (John 15:18-20, NLT).

Jesus often warned his disciples that persecution would come. And it did, first from fellow Jews, then from the Roman Empire. As the disciples carried on his ministry, a tide of resentment, hatred, and open opposition rose. Eleven of the original twelve apostles met violent deaths. In a few years, the megalomaniacal emperor Nero rose to power. Because Christians refused to worship Nero as "Almighty God" and "Savior," he blamed them for the burning of

Rome in AD 64 and instigated three and a half years of persecution that claimed the lives of thousands of Christians. According to Josephus, a first-century Jewish historian working for Rome, Christians were thrown to the lions, beheaded, and even burned alive to give light to Roman revelries at night. However, this type of persecution isn't relegated to the past.

Today, Christians are the single-most persecuted religious group in the world. Worldwide each month 322 Christians are killed for their faith, 214 churches and Christian properties are destroyed, and 772 forms of violence (such as beatings, abductions, rapes, and arrests) are committed against Christians. According to the U.S. Department of State, Christians in more than sixty countries face persecution from their governments or surrounding neighbors simply because of their belief in Jesus Christ.[6] In North America, violence against Christians is rare, but the modern transition from living in a majority Christian nation to an increasingly pluralistic, religiously diverse country is challenging at times. And Christians haven't always responded the best way. Persecution, whether real or perceived, can often stir a desire for revenge or retaliation.

Magneto can teach us something about that. Erik Lehnsherr, also known as Magneto, is one of the world's most powerful mutants and the X-Men's most dangerous foe. As a young Jewish boy living in 1940s Poland, Erik experienced persecution firsthand when Nazi soldiers forcibly separated him from his parents and imprisoned him in the Auschwitz concentration camp. Unlike his parents, Erik survived the war, but he never forgot the experience.

Decades later, Erik's past experience convinces him that humans and mutants can never peacefully coexist, and that war is inevitable. In *X-Men: The Last Stand*, Magneto attends a mutant rally in an attempt to recruit warriors for his war. "Make no mistake, my brothers," he announces within the echoing cathedral of an abandoned church, "they will draw first blood.... The only question is, will you join my brotherhood and fight or wait for the inevitable genocide? Who will you stand with, the humans or us?" Magneto's militant response to the persecution of mutants results in conflict and casualties for both mutants and humans alike.[7]

No wonder, then, that Jesus taught his disciples to respond to their enemies with love, not reactionary hatred or retaliatory violence. Christians, like comic book mutants, must learn a better way to respond when the world hates us. The X-men reveal that better way.

A POWERFUL PEOPLE

Each of the X-Men enjoys extraordinary mutant abilities. Among the iconic members, Cyclops emits powerful energy beams from his eyes, Jean Grey wields telekinetic abilities, Storm controls the weather, and Wolverine brandishes retractable claws and boasts a remarkable rate of healing. Other mutants can walk through walls, teleport, or even control other people's minds. But despite the persecution and hatred levied against them, Professor Xavier instructs his students to use their mutant powers for the betterment of humankind—to be heroes not just to their fellow mutants, but to all people. As such, the X-Men often find themselves using their extraordinary abilities to defend and rescue the very people who persecute them, such as Senator Kelly in the first X-Men movie.

Jesus gave similar instructions to his followers: "You have heard that it was said, 'Love your neighbor and hate your enemy.' But I tell you, love your enemies and pray for those who persecute you" (Matthew 5:43-44, NIV).

This passage reminds me of a familiar preachers' story about a reporter interviewing an old man on his one-hundredth birthday. "What are you most proud of?" the reporter asked. "Well," said the man, "I don't have an enemy in the world." Smiling, the reporter replied, "What a beautiful thought. How inspirational!" "Yep," added the centenarian, "I outlived every last one of them!" Rather than outliving our enemies, Jesus calls us to *out-love* our enemies.

Few Marvel mutants know the sting of persecution better than Nightcrawler. Also known as Kurt Wagner, Nightcrawler first leapt from comics to cartoons in a 1995 episode of X-Men. In a Transylvania-like village set in the snowy hills of Bavaria, a team of X-men—Wolverine, Rogue, and Gambit—responds to reports of a blue-skinned, pointy-tailed demon terrorizing the locals. Upon investigation, the team discovers that the so-called demon is, in fact, a mutant receiving shelter from a small group of monks in a modest monastery. Nightcrawler explains that, unlike most mutants, his condition was obvious from birth. His devilish appearance frightened all who saw him. "I was an outcast," Kurt recalls, "shunned and hated."

"Don't it make you crazy?" Wolverine commiserates.

"It did once," Nightcrawler agrees, "But then I found peace, by devoting my life to God. He directed me to this place, where they value the character of my heart, not my appearance."

"Don't talk to me about God," Wolverine snaps. Looking deject-edly at the razor-sharp claws protruding from his fists, Wolverine questions Nightcrawler, "What kind of God would allow men to do this to me?"

"Our ability to understand God's purposes is *limited*, but we take comfort in the fact that his love is *limitless*," Kurt expounds.

Moments later, an angry mob of townspeople, toting torches and wielding weapons, storms the monastery in search of the supposed demon. "Heartless fools. They know not what they do," Nightcrawler laments in an echo of Jesus' words on the cross. In the midst of the madness, the monastery is set ablaze, and the townsfolk witness Nightcrawler risking his life to save theirs. Kurt's heroism softens the hearts of the townspeople, and they no longer look upon him with fear and hatred.

Wolverine's heart similarly softens. In the aftermath of the fire, Nightcrawler rescues a slightly scorched Bible from the charred remains. Handing it to Wolverine, he says, "Here, I've marked a few passages you may find rewarding." The episode ends with Wolverine kneeling in a cathedral in nearby Paris, praying and reading Scripture.[8]

Because Kurt Wagner chose to love his enemies and pray for his persecutors, he not only won the hearts of the townsfolk but also won the soul of his fellow mutant.

This is why Jesus calls us to love our enemies and pray for those who persecute us. Love and prayer are extraordinary abilities. In fact, Jesus once said the distinguishing mark of his followers would be their love: "By this everyone will know that you are my disciples, if you love one another" (John 13:35, NIV).

What makes us peculiar and what supplies our power to overcome both persecution (and the temptation to become persecutors of others) is not our faith or convictions, as important as those are. It is love—God's love for us in Christ and our love for others because of God's love for us. We worship a God who wants us to conquer his enemies by loving them and welcoming them into his family. Love and prayer are our most powerful weapons in winning hateful hearts to Jesus.

* * *

Stan Lee said, "That was the underlining philosophy behind [the X-Men]...to try and show the reader the irony and the fallacy of being against the very people who are trying to help you and do something good."[9] Like the X-Men, Christians are peculiar. We're peculiar because we no longer belong to this world. As a result, we have encountered persecution, and in turn, we have been tempted to strike out at our enemies. But we are empowered to follow the example of the X-Men and the example of Jesus, using the power of love to help lead people to Jesus himself—the only hero who can truly save us all.

NOTES

1. *X-Men*, directed by Brian Singer (20th Century Fox, 2000), DVD special features.

2. *X-Men: First Class*, directed by Matthew Vaughn (20th Century Fox, 2011).

3. *X-Men: The Last Stand*, directed by Brett Ratner (20th Century Fox, 2006).

4. "Peculiar," *Dictionary.com*, http://dictionary.reference.com/browse/peculiar?s=t.

5. Mikhail Lyubansky, "The Racial Politics of X-Men: Can Anti-Mutant Oppression Teach Us Something about Racism?" *Psychology Today*, June 5, 2011, https://www.psychologytoday.com/blog/between-the-lines/201106/the-racial-politics-x-men.

6. Open *Doors*, "Christian Persecution," <https://www.opendoorsusa.org/christian-persecution/>.

7. *X-Men: The Last Stand*, directed by Brett Ratner (20th Century Fox, 2006).

8. "Nightcrawler," *X-Men: The Animated Series* #52 (Fox Kids Network, 1995).

9. *X-Men*, directed by Brian Singer (20th Century Fox, 2000), DVD special features.

SCOTT ARMORS UP AS THE MOVIE VERSION OF IRON MAN!

PHOTO BY ASHLEY BAYLES

11
IRON MAN

Marvel Studio's first box office blockbuster introduced audiences to Tony Stark, a genius inventor and billionaire owner of the technology company Stark Industries. Tony made much of his fortune by designing weapons for the military, until the day a terrorist organization, known as the Ten Rings, kidnapped him and coerced him to build them a weapon of mass destruction. Rather than build the weapon, however, Stark secretly built a suit of armor to help him escape.[1] Inside his armor, Tony Stark became what creator Stan Lee originally dubbed the Invincible Iron Man.

Experiencing Iron Man's cinematic debut still looms large in my memory. My wife, Ashley, accompanied me to the theater, and our then two-year-old son occupied the seat between us. His excitement rivaled my own as we waited at the concession stand and searched for a seat, but about forty minutes into the movie his enthusiasm propelled him right out of his seat.

As Tony's dramatic escape scene drew to a close, he pulled the ignition on his steel suit and rocketed into the air. Just then, my son launched out of his seat shouting, "Iron Man flies!" His enthusiasm infected other moviegoers and made the whole cinema experience more enjoyable for everyone.

As we exited the theater that night, my mind immediately began devising plans to fabricate my own Iron Man armor. After doing some Internet research, I discovered that other enthusiastic fans had already been enjoying some success with sculpting or what cosplayers call "scratch building" (using cardboard or other similar materials, without a template), but the most common and preferred method of replicating Tony's armor was Pepakura, which is a Japanese word for "paper craft." Reminiscent of origami, Pepakura models start off as 3D computer images and then unfold into 2D patterns that can be constructed from cardstock or foam. The process seemed difficult and daunting. As much as I wanted an Iron Man suit, I put the project on the back burner. Marvel's *Iron Man* movie franchise enjoyed two sequels before I worked up the nerve to tackle the project.

I finally committed to start work on it early in 2014. The process dragged on for more than three weeks and ate up more hours than I can remember, but in the end it was worth it! I debuted my armor that April at Cape Comic-Con in Cape Girardeau, Missouri. Ashley joined me as Black Widow, and the kids (we had three of them by then!) cosplayed as various Avengers. Iron Man helped draw quite a crowd to our Costumers for Christ table and enabled us to share the gospel with more than three hundred people that day!

For those of you who aren't familiar with the story of Iron Man: not only did Tony escape captivity, but also he continued using his armor to fight evil and injustice. Outside of his armor, the human inventor Tony Stark is vulnerable, but inside his hi-tech Iron Man suit, he's virtually invincible.

Unlike Iron Man, you and I don't battle terrorists or super-villains in a hi-tech suit of armor. But like Iron Man, we do have a battle to fight, and as Christians, we've been given a suit of armor that makes us invincible against our enemy. Listen to what God's Word has to say about that:

A final word: Be strong in the Lord and in his mighty power. Put on all of God's armor so that you will be able to stand firm against all strategies of the devil. For we are not fighting against flesh-and-blood enemies, but against evil rulers and authorities of the unseen world, against mighty powers in this dark world, and against evil spirits in the heavenly places. Therefore, put on every piece of God's armor so you will be able to resist the enemy in the time of evil. Then after the battle you will still be standing firm. Stand your ground, putting on the belt of truth and the body armor of God's righteousness. For shoes, put on the peace that comes from the Good News so that you will be fully prepared. In addition to all of these, hold up the shield of faith to stop the fiery arrows of the devil. Put on salvation as your helmet, and take the sword of the Spirit, which is the word of God. (Ephesians 6:10-17, NLT)

Paul's analogy provides a dramatic connection with Iron Man's story, including a detailed comparison between Tony Stark's hi-tech suit of armor and the spiritual armor of God, and underscores three aspects of our Christian battle.

OUR ADVERSARY

In the film, Iron Man's chief adversary masquerades as Tony's business partner and friend, Obadiah Stane. When Tony's father and founder of Stark Industries, Howard Stark, died in a tragic car accident, Howard's lifelong friend and ally, Obadiah Stane, gained control of Stark Industries. His leadership was short-lived, however, as Tony inherited the company on his twenty-first birthday. Tony ushered in a new era for Stark Industries, creating smarter weapons and advanced robotics, while Obadiah was demoted and dispatched to Tony's shadow. Publically and personally, Obadiah pretended to be Tony's biggest fan and best friend. But beneath his smiling exterior, Obadiah seethed with jealousy and hatred.

The movie reveals that Stane secretly orchestrated Tony's abduction. When Tony escapes captivity, Stane again works behind the scenes to convince the Stark Industries board of directors to file an injunction against him, removing Tony as CEO. Ultimately, Stane steals Tony's Iron Man designs, creates his own suit of armor, and sets out to destroy his rival.

Christians face a similar adversary. The Bible calls him the devil or Satan (the word *Satan* is Hebrew and means "adversary"). The apostle Paul cautioned early believers to "stand firm against the schemes of the devil" (Ephesians 6:11, NASB). Like Obadiah Stane, the devil works behind the scenes, scheming and plotting ways to destroy Christians and sever our relationship with God. And just as Stane coordinated Tony's capture, the devil uses deception to ensnare hearts and minds. Elsewhere Paul warned, "Gently instruct those who oppose the truth. Perhaps God will change those people's hearts, and they will learn the truth. Then they will come to their senses and escape from the devil's trap. For they have been held captive by him to do whatever he wants" (2 Timothy 2:25-26, NLT).

While Christians differ in our understanding of how exactly our adversary works and what it means to struggle "against the spiritual forces of evil in the heavenly realms" (Ephesians 6:12, NIV), the New Testament makes clear that the devil is a sinister adversary. The apostle Peter likewise warned, "Be serious! Be alert! Your adversary the Devil is prowling around like a roaring lion, looking for anyone he can devour" (1 Peter 5:8, HCSB).

As Christians, we need to take this adversary seriously. At the same time, a proper perspective on spiritual skirmishes focuses not on the schemes of Satan, but on the supremacy of God. Much like Tony Stark's armor enabled him to overcome his adversary, the armor of God does the same for us.

OUR ARMOR

Tony's original armor suit was a clunky tin can constructed out of spare parts in a cave. After escaping captivity, however, Tony improved his designs, creating the sleek, sophisticated, red and gold armor that's become a comic book icon. Of course, being a billionaire genius engineer, Tony constantly makes improvements and upgrades to his armor. The Mark XLII (42), the predominantly gold-colored armor featured in *Iron Man 3*, is constructed of an advanced titanium alloy and reinforced with silicon-infused steel and ceramic plating, which makes Tony virtually indestructible. The armor contains powerful flight and navigation systems as well as an impressive array of weapons, including repulsors rays and a uni-beam powered by Tony's arc-reactor. Although it may not be as shiny or space-agey as Tony's, the armor of God, when worn properly, makes its wearer more invincible than Iron Man.

Unlike most superheroes, Iron Man doesn't need a belt; his suit of armor is held in place with nuts and bolts. A Christian's armor, however, is held together by the belt of truth. The truth in this context refers to integrity, a life of practical truthfulness and honesty. Jesus described our spiritual adversary, the devil, saying, "When he lies, he speaks his native language, for he is a liar and the father of lies" (John 8:44, NIV). When we lie, we follow in the devil's footsteps. A life of honesty and truthfulness is our first line of defense against the strategies of Satan.

The centerpiece of Iron Man's breastplate is his arc-reactor, which not only powers his suit but also keeps him alive. When Tony was being abducted by the terrorists, an explosion embedded shrapnel deep into his chest, and the small metal shards slowly worked their way toward his heart. In the movie, one of Stark's fellow captives called him "the walking dead," because the shrapnel would soon penetrate his heart and kill him. In designing his armor, Tony implanted a powerful electromagnet in his chest that attracts the shrapnel, preventing it from crawling any deeper. If his arc-reactor were shut off, those shards of metal would again creep toward his heart and ultimately kill him.

In much the same way, the breastplate of righteousness protects our hearts. Put simply, righteousness involves doing what's right in God's eyes. By making godly decisions and doing the right thing in any given situation, we protect our hearts from spiritual attacks. Without the righteousness of God guarding our hearts, we're just as vulnerable as Iron Man without his arc-reactor.

Just as Iron Man's rocket-propelled boots carry him off on his missions, the footwear of the gospel of peace suggests that we need to advance into enemy territory, always prepared to share the gospel—a message of peace and restoration with God—with a world ravaged by conflict. (Later in this book, Wonder Woman will teach us a little more about this mission of peace.)

Unlike his fellow Avenger Captain America, Iron Man doesn't carry a literal shield, yet his armor shields him from nearly any attack. Likewise, the Christian's shield of faith offers protection against all the fiery darts of our adversary. We'll come back to the shield of faith in the next chapter, but know for now that our faith, when placed in God, becomes an indestructible shield around our souls. Faith is essential in surviving spiritual struggles.

While protecting his head from injury, Iron Man's helmet also contains a digital heads-up display that keeps important information right in front of Tony's eyes. The helmet of salvation can serve the same purpose for us. It reminds us that we have a Savior—a Holy Hero who gave his life to save us and give us eternal life. If you are convinced that you have a Holy Hero, then you have a limitless capacity for hope, and you'll have compassion for others who are in need of such a Hero.

Finally, although Iron Man's armor is equipped with an assortment of offensive weapons, the armor of God provides just one: "the sword of the Spirit, which is the word of God" (Ephesians

6:17, NIV). Elsewhere, the Bible describes itself as a two-edged sword (Hebrews 4:12), useful for both offense and defense. Jesus himself teaches us how to wield this weapon. Preparing for his public ministry, Jesus spent forty days alone in the wilderness. Isolated and hungry, Jesus was at his most vulnerable. That's when Satan attacked. The Bible records three specific temptations that the devil dangled in front of Jesus. Yet, each time Jesus responded with the same words, "It is written..." (Matthew 4:4, 7, 10), and then he proceeded to quote Scripture to Satan.

No matter what situation you're faced with, God's Word will speak to that issue. Let God's Word speak to you—words of affirmation and encouragement, hope and humility, power and peace, joy and justice. Memorize some verses that relate to your life and struggles. Then, when the adversary strikes, respond immediately by speaking God's Word aloud from your arsenal of Scriptures.

Without the full armor of God, our hearts and souls are vulnerable to enemy attack, but with it, "We are pressed on every side by troubles, but we are not crushed. We are perplexed, but not driven to despair. We are hunted down, but never abandoned by God. We get knocked down, but we are not destroyed" (2 Corinthians 4:8-9, NLT). In other words, in the armor of God, we become invincible.

Of course, Iron Man's armor alone doesn't secure his status as hero. In addition to his armor, Tony faces down his adversaries with an unwavering attitude.

OUR ATTITUDE

When Tony's love interest and personal assistant, Pepper Pots, discovers that Stark and Iron Man are one and the same, she tries talking him out of his newfound mission and even threatens to quit. "You stood by my side all these years," Tony replies, "while I reaped the benefits of destruction. Now that I'm trying to protect the people I've put in harm's way, you're going to walk out?"

Pepper responds, "You're going to kill yourself, Tony. I'm not going to be a part of it."

"I shouldn't be alive," Tony confesses, "unless it was for a reason. I'm not crazy, Pepper. I just finally know what I have to do. And I know in my heart that it's right."[2]

No longer obsessed with power, pleasure, or possessions, Tony discovered the value of standing up for others and standing against the forces of evil. He wouldn't let anyone—not even Pepper—convince him to give up.

Christians are called to demonstrate the same steadfast attitude. Paul began this section of Scripture saying, "Finally, be strong in the Lord…so that you can take your stand" (Ephesians 6:10-11, NIV). Again he says, "That is why you need to put on God's full armor. Then on the day of evil you will be able to stand strong. And when you have finished the whole fight, you will still be standing" (Ephesians 6:13, NCV). Stand strong, Paul urges. Hold your ground!

Captain America expressed a similar sentiment. In a Marvel Comics crossover event, *Civil War*, which combines characters from different comic series, ideological differences drove a wedge between Iron Man and Captain America. Lines were drawn. Sides were chosen. In the midst of the conflicts and confrontations, Spider-Man struggles to choose a side. At first he agrees with Iron Man, but then Captain America makes an impassioned plea:

> Doesn't matter what the press says. Doesn't matter what politicians or the mob say. Doesn't matter if the whole country decides something wrong is something right. This nation was founded on one principle above all else: the requirement that we stand up for what we believe, no matter the odds or the consequences. When the mob and the press and the whole world tell you to move, your job is to plant your feet like a tree beside the river of truth, and tell the whole world—No. You move.[3]

Captain America describes exactly the attitude that we must embrace in the realm of spiritual struggles. Our adversary is relentless in his assaults. We must be resolute in our stand against him. Souls are at stake. To let down our guard is to invite spiritual defeat. If we give in to Satan's schemes even an inch—if we listen to his lies, if we compromise our convictions, if we abandon our faith, or lose sight of our salvation—we'll lose the battle. Let's be strong in the Lord. Put on the full armor of God. Take a stand.

***

My son is still an enthusiastic Iron Man fan. Recently, I even built him his very own armor out of EVA foam and hot glue, featuring the patriotic paint job of Iron Man's sidekick, Iron Patriot. Each time we suit up, he and I both are visually reminded of our sinister adversary, our spiritual armor, and the stalwart attitude that we must embrace in order to achieve spiritual victory.

Maybe you're in the middle of a spiritual battle right now. Maybe you're feeling particularly vulnerable to the devil's attacks. Whatever your struggle, I urge you to take up the full armor of God and take a stand.

NOTES

1. *Iron Man*, directed by Jon Favreau (Paramount Pictures, 2008).

2. Ibid.

3. J. Michael Straczynski (writer) and Ron Garney (artist), "Civil War," *Amazing Spider-Man* #13 (Marvel Comics, 2007).

12
CAPTAIN AMERICA

Monogamy is important to many comic book buffs. Most comic collectors remain loyal to one of two publishers: Marvel or DC. For the better part of my life, I was a DC man. The comic book boxes crammed into my childhood closet brimmed over with the likes of Superman, Batman, Flash, Green Lantern, Wonder Woman, and other icons exclusive to DC Comics. Among the many talented writers and artists who worked on those books, none was better than Dan Jurgens. Having written and drawn Superman for the better part of a decade, Mr. Jurgens earned my unwavering allegiance. Even when he killed Superman at the diabolical hands of Doomsday, I loved every page that he scribbled and scripted. But then came the day that Dan Jurgens departed DC and loaned his talents to the "other guys."

After leaving DC, Dan began writing, and eventually drawing, Marvel's new Captain America book. I missed seeing his unique art style gracing the pages of my favorite comics, but a few months later, while on my weekly excursion to the comic book store, the striking cover of *Captain America* #40 caught my eye. The familiar star-spangled costume never looked better.

It felt wrong at first. Almost like cheating on a girlfriend. But if Dan Jurgens could write and draw Captain America for Marvel

Comics, then maybe I could buy just one issue. *No one would have to know*, I told myself. In time, I collected Dan's complete run on the series and, eventually, the entire series. I couldn't help but love it. As Stan Lee once said, "Captain America is the very definition of a superhero."[1]

Nearly a decade later, just as Cap was my first Marvel comic, he also became my first Marvel cosplay. I'll never forget my first time costuming as Captain America. Just one year after my very first attempt at costume creating, my family and I returned to Metropolis on a sweltering and sunny afternoon in June 2009. I still wasn't in the best of shape, and my costume needed a little improvement, but as I paraded down the main road, star-studded shield in tow, a little boy—no more than four years old—appeared out of nowhere, wrapped his arms tightly around my legs, and announced, "I love you, Captain America!" He vanished as quickly as he appeared, but I knew in that instant that I would be costuming for years to come.

The story of Captain America is really the story of Steve Rogers, a skinny kid from Brooklyn, New York. Despite his scrawny shape and sickly health, Steve volunteered for a top-secret military experiment dubbed Operation Rebirth. Choosing Steve because of his altruistic and patriotic heart, military scientists injected Steve with a special serum and bombarded him with "Vita-Rays," which transformed him from a frail young man to the peak of human perfection—the super-soldier, Captain America. Imbued with enhanced strength, speed, and agility, Captain America became the Sentinel of Liberty as he defended freedom against the Nazis. Then, after being lost in the Arctic and frozen in ice for decades, he was found and thawed out by the Avengers and continues to fight by their sides as a man out of time.

The story of Steve Rogers—an unlikely underdog transformed into a victorious hero—rings familiar not just because it's a favorite of comic book creators, but because it's our story too. In the Bible, God frequently converted the most unlikely candidates into mighty heroes. He still does so today. The fictional tale of Captain America mirrors the Christian life in multiple ways.

WE ARE CHOSEN

Surprisingly, Steve is chosen for this special privilege not for his strength, but for his weakness. In *Captain America: The First Avenger*, Colonel Chester Phillips challenges Dr. Erskine's choice, "You're not really thinking about picking Rogers, are you?" Erskine replies, "I am more than just thinking about it. He is the clear choice." Flabbergasted, Phillips retorts, "When you brought a ninety pound asthmatic onto my army base, I let it slide. I thought, what the hell? Maybe he'll be useful to you, like a gerbil. I never thought you'd pick him!"[2]

Curious, isn't it? Why would Dr. Abraham Erskine choose the most frail and feeble candidate available? Steve wonders the same thing. The night before the procedure that transforms him into Captain America, Steve asks the good doctor, "Why me?" Erskine explains, "This is why you were chosen. Because a strong man, who has known power all his life, will lose respect for that power. But a weak man knows the value of strength, and knows compassion."

God tends to make similar choices for similar reasons. When sending Samuel in search of a new king, God warned, "Don't judge by his appearance or height…. The LORD doesn't see things the way you see them. People judge by outward appearance, but the LORD looks at the heart" (1 Samuel 16:7, NLT). God isn't interested in people of great power, position, or prestige by worldly standards; rather, God seeks out those who are humble in heart—the meek, the lowly, the oppressed, the poor.

God loves the little guys. Moses assured the Israelites of this when he said, "The LORD did not set his heart on you and choose you because you were more numerous than other nations, for you were the smallest of all nations!" (Deuteronomy 7:7, NLT).

In Judges 6, we're introduced to Gideon. It was wartime, and Gideon was hiding when an angel of the Lord appeared to tell him that he would be the one to restore the faith and freedom of Israel. Imagine Gideon's astonishment as he declared, "How and with what could I ever save Israel? Look at me. My clan's the weakest in Manasseh and I'm the runt of the litter" (Judges 6:15, MSG).

For seven years Gideon grew accustomed to being bullied and beat up. A nomadic tribe known as the Midianites would wait until the Israelites had harvested their crops and raised their cattle, and then swoop down and raid their farms, stealing what they could and destroying the rest. They were the quintessential neighborhood bullies. Gideon was a loser in his own eyes. But that didn't stop God. The Lord chose Gideon anyway and transformed him into a mighty man of valor—a hero to God's people and to his own tribe. What God did for Gideon, he can do for you.

The New Testament explains, "God chose... the weak things of the world to shame the strong. He chose what the world thinks is unimportant and what the world looks down on and thinks is nothing in order to destroy what the world thinks is important. God did this so that no one can brag in his presence" (1 Corinthians 1:27-29, NCV).

Perhaps you can identify with Steve Rogers or Gideon. Maybe you've looked in the mirror and seen a frail failure or the runt of the litter. You're not the strongest, smartest, or most successful person you know. But that's okay. If you're accustomed to being beat up, picked on, overlooked, or underrated, I've got good news for you! God loves the long shots, the losers, and the little guys. God seeks out men and women with humble hearts—hearts that say, "Lord, I'm a nobody. I'm nothing without you. Will you use me?" When God finds such a heart, something extraordinary happens. God changes it. Like Steve Rogers, those who give their lives to Jesus are in for a change.

WE ARE CHANGED

Jesus once cautioned his inner circle, "The spirit is willing, but the flesh is weak" (Mark 14:38, NIV). He could have easily said the same thing to Steve Rogers. Scrawny Steve longed to enlist and aid in the war effort, but due to a sickly and skinny physique, Steve repeatedly failed the physical requirements for service.

After being chosen for Operation Rebirth and injected with Erskine's formula, however, Steve transformed into the perfect physical specimen, stronger and more agile than an Olympic athlete. Suddenly, Steve's weak and wimpy frame morphed into a barrel chest, broad shoulders, and bulging biceps. Now able to run a mile in 73 seconds and bench-press up to 1,200 pounds, Steve Rogers changed from a wiry weakling into America's first super-soldier.

Jesus wants to do the same thing to you. Well, not exactly the same thing. Unlike Steve, our transformation isn't physical; it's spiritual. When believers embrace Jesus as their Holy Hero, a change begins. When Christ gets into your heart and life, a transformation takes place. The Bible puts it this way: "Don't copy the behavior and customs of this world, but let God transform you into a new person by changing the way you think. Then you will learn to know God's will for you, which is good and pleasing and perfect" (Romans 12:2, NLT).

God wants to change you. The Lord wants to make you into a better you. Don't get me wrong—God loves you just the way you are. But God also loves you too much to leave you that way. The Lord wants to bring about radical spiritual transformation in your life that begins by changing the way you think, and then spreads to your attitudes and actions.

So what does this transformation look like? Paul created a comparison chart in his letter to the Galatian churches. He wrote,

> When you follow the desires of your sinful nature, the results are very clear: sexual immorality, impurity, lustful pleasures, idolatry, sorcery, hostility, quarreling, jealousy, outbursts of anger, selfish ambition, dissension, division, envy, drunkenness, wild parties, and other sins like these…. But the Holy Spirit produces this kind of fruit in our lives: love, joy, peace, patience, kindness, goodness, faithfulness, gentleness, and self-control. (Galatians 5:19-23, NLT)

Sin and selfishness come naturally for us. Somewhere on Paul's list I'm sure you see the sins that have plagued your past. If not, certainly "other sins like these" come to mind. But, as we learned from Superman, Jesus died to pay the penalty for our sins. And, as we learned from Black Widow, he wiped out all the red in my ledger and yours, providing us a fresh start. Even after all this, however, we're still sinners at heart. We have a propensity for evil and immorality. So when we receive Jesus as our Savior, he infuses us with his Holy Spirit.

Just as Erskine's formula coursing through his veins transformed Steve from the inside out, the Holy Spirit flowing through us begins to change our hearts and minds. The Spirit of God dwelling inside us produces healthy and holy fruit in our lives—love, joy, peace, patience, kindness, good, faithfulness, gentleness, and self-control. In other words, the Spirit of God works within us to make us more like the Son of God. The Bible puts it this way: "And the Lord—who is the Spirit—makes us more and more like him as we are changed into his glorious image" (2 Corinthians 3:18, NLT). God's ultimate goal for your life is to transform you into the spitting image of Jesus.

Pastor and author Robert J. Morgan once explained the words in 2 Corinthians 3:18 by telling the story of a heavyset woman who went to an exercise and diet clinic. He writes, "The first thing the supervisor did was draw a silhouette on a mirror in the shape she wished to become. As she stood before the mirror, her reflected shape bulged out over the silhouette. The instructor told her, 'Our goal is for you to fit this shape.' For weeks the woman dieted and exercised. Each week she would stand in front of the mirror, but her volume, while decreasing, still overflowed. And so she exercised harder and dieted more rigidly. Finally one day, to everyone's delight, as she stood in front of the mirror she was conformed to the image of the silhouette."[3]

It would be wonderful if we experienced the same kind of instantaneous transformation as Steve Rogers, but it takes time and trust in the work of the Spirit to be conformed to the image of God's Son. Through the discipline of prayer and patience, the Spirit trims away the sin in our lives. Through the exercise of belief, Bible study, and obedience, the Spirit gives us spiritual muscles that we didn't know even existed. Spiritual transformation is a gradual, lifelong process that will be finished only when we get to heaven. The Bible says, "We have not yet been shown what we will be in the future. But we know that when Christ comes again, we will be like him" (1 John 3:2, NCV). What a glorious day that will be!

WE ARE CHARGED

After Captain America rescues a captured platoon from a weapons facility thirty miles behind enemy lines, Colonel Phillips charges him with defeating the Nazi science division, Hydra, and their leader, Red Skull. Accompanied by a ragtag band of soldiers known as the Howlin' Commandos, Captain America leads the charge against Red Skull and his cult-like followers. While Hydra wields advanced weaponry based on Asgardian technology, Captain America carries only one weapon: a special shield made from an indestructible alloy capable of absorbing kinetic energy. Victory after victory, Captain

America cuts a swath of destruction through Hydra's forces and finally foils their plans for global domination.

As we learned from Iron Man, God issues a similar charge to Christians: "Take up the shield of faith, with which you can extinguish all the flaming arrows of the evil one" (Ephesians 6:16, NIV). Like Captain America, Christians are embroiled in battle. Our adversary brandishes a vast array of flaming arrows, yet each one is quenched on impact against the shield of faith.

In the comics, Captain America's shield is made of an alloy composed of three metals. The first is vibranium, a rare vibration-absorbing metal found only in the jungles of Wakanda. Second is adamantium, the same indestructible metal that Wolverine's claws and bones are coated in. Finally, in the story *Fear Itself*, Asgardian blacksmiths added some of the mystical metal Uru to the shield, the same stuff from which Thor's magical hammer was forged.[4] These three metals combine to make Captain America's shield utterly unique and totally indestructible.

A Christian's shield of faith is similarly indestructible, not because of the strength of our faith, but because of the object of our faith: God. In the words of David, "The LORD is my strength and my shield; my heart trusts in him, and he helps me" (Psalm 28:7, NIV).

In *Captain America* #2, Cap faces the daunting task of rescuing an entire crew of a submerged naval submarine hijacked by Hydra. After witnessing Captain America take down several Hydra agents with a single throw of his shield, Lieutenant Commander Rebecca Houston asks, "How'd you get so good with that thing?" Rogers explains that years of constant practice have evolved into pure instinct. "I depend on it like nothing else in this world," Steve says, "Don't know what I'd do without it." Later he concocts a plan of escape that involves launching Houston and himself through a torpedo tube with only his shield between them and the blast. As Captain America crouches into the tube with his arms around the nervous lieutenant, he assures her, "Trust the shield. It's never let me down before."[5]

The same is true of God. When we learn to trust in the Lord the way Captain America trusts his shield, we'll never be let down. No enemy will ever defeat us. When our hearts trust in God, he becomes our strength and shield, an ever-present help in times of trouble.

***

Like Steve Rogers, you and I have been chosen despite—and possibly even because of—our weakness. We're being changed by God, our Heavenly Father, conformed to the image of his perfect Son. And we're charged by God to fight the good fight of faith, armed with the shield of faith. God specializes in transforming zeroes into heroes. Our Savior seeks out the losers, the long shots, and the little guys, and turns us into mighty men and women of valor. If you'll let him, Jesus will do the same for you.

NOTES

1. Neversoft Entertainment, *Spider-Man* (Activision, 2000), PlayStation.

2. *Captain America: The First Avenger*, directed by Joe Johnston (Paramount Pictures, 2011).

3. Robert J. Morgan, *Nelson's Complete Book of Stories, Illustrations & Quotes* (Nashville: Thomas Nelson, 2000), 103–4.

4. Matt Fraction (writer) and Stuart Immonen (artist), "Thor's Day," *Fear Itself* #7 (Marvel Comics, 2011).

5. Mark Waid (writer) and Ron Garney (artist), "To Serve and Protect," *Captain America* #2 (Marvel Comics, 1998).

FELLOW COSTUMERS FOR CHRIST, JOHN WES CRITCHLOW AND SANTINO MARANI, COSTUME AS ARROW AND HIS DEADLY NEMESIS DEATHSTROKE.

PHOTO BY MARK SHAFER

13
GREEN ARROW

Until recently, Green Arrow remained one of DC Comics's lesser-known superheroes. Much like the legendary Robin Hood or Marvel's Hawkeye, Green Arrow battles evildoers with a quiver full of trick arrows and a keen eye.

The CW Network's hit television show *Arrow* recently introduced the comic book character to mainstream audiences. A fresh, live-action take on DC's emerald archer, *Arrow* features a gloomier, grittier version of the once-campy character. More than three million fans tuned in to watch Green Arrow's action-packed adventures in the first season, making *Arrow* the CW's highest-rated new series in the past five years. Thanks to the popularity of the new series, multitudes of Green Arrow costumes can be seen at comic book conventions and other costumed events.

I first cosplayed as Green Arrow in 2012, prior to the leather-clad look of the television series. I modeled my costume on Green Arrow's classic comic book appearance designed by legendary artist Neal Adams in 1969. My wife accompanied me as Green Arrow's long-time love interest and fellow superhero, Dinah Lance, also known as Black Canary.

Although my Green Arrow comic collection is limited, Ashley and I enjoy watching Arrow's action-packed adventures on television, and I find myself enthralled by his story. Spoiled billionaire playboy Oliver Queen disappears when his yacht is lost at sea. He returns five years later a changed man, determined to clean up his city as a hooded vigilante armed with a bow and arrows.

Green Arrow reminds me of another pampered rich kid we read about in the Bible. His name is Joseph. Like Oliver Queen, he came from a wealthy family and a life of ease, but adversity changed all that. Trouble found Joseph and left him a changed man. Interestingly, the stories of these two young men—one fictitious, the other factual—intersect at multiple points.

SEASON OF SUFFERING

Oliver Queen lived an extravagant life fixated on women and wild parties. Setting sail on his father's yacht for an entertaining excursion, Oliver never expected to wind up shipwrecked and stranded on a treacherous island for the next five years. But that's what happened. In *Arrow*'s modern retelling of Oliver's comic book origins, seeing his girlfriend disappear into the ocean and his father shoot himself in desperation only marked the beginning of Oliver's troubles. Washed ashore on a deserted island, Oliver struggled to survive. Things went from bad to worse when Oliver discovered that he wasn't alone. A group of mercenaries scoured the island for an ancient secret, capturing or killing anyone who might get in their way.

Raised in the lap of luxury, then exiled in an unfamiliar land with danger all around—if anyone could relate to Oliver's ordeal, Joseph could. Joseph grew up enjoying extravagant life as well. The youngest of twelve brothers, Joseph was favored by their father above all the rest, which he demonstrated through lavish gifts, including a famous "coat of many colours" (KJV). The Bible says, "Jacob loved Joseph more than any of his other children.... So one day Jacob had a special gift made for Joseph—a beautiful robe" (Genesis 37:3, NLT).

122

Of course, this stirred up envy and hatred in his older brothers' hearts. One day, they finally had had enough. The brothers gang up on Joseph. They strip him of his dignity and his beautiful coat and throw him into an empty well. Eventually, they sell him to a group of traveling merchants who, in turn, sell him as slave in Egypt. Far from home, surrounded by danger in a strange land, Joseph struggled through his own season of suffering.

Oliver's suffering came in the form of a shipwreck. Joseph's came in the form of slavery. But the sad truth is, everyone suffers. Jesus promised, "In this world you will have trouble" (John 16:33, NIV). Someone once said, "Trouble is like home. Either you're there, going to it, or coming from it."

It reminds me of an Army chaplain who posted this sign on his door: "If you have troubles, come in and tell me all about them. If you don't have troubles, come in and tell me how you do it." Maybe your suffering came in the form of a diagnosis, divorce papers, insurmountable debt, or the death of someone you love. Maybe you're suffering from abuse, abandonment, or addiction.

Suffering, struggle, and sadness seem to be hardwired into the world. Let's face it: bad things happen. They happen with unpredictable frequency and fluctuating levels of intensity. Some are mere inconveniences; others are life-shattering catastrophes. The question is this: how will you respond when trouble finds you? When suffering strikes, how we respond reveals the strength of our resolve and steadiness of our faith. For both Oliver and Joseph, their season of suffering became a season of sharpening.

SEASON OF SHARPENING

Stranded on a remote tropical island, Oliver Queen had only one goal: survival. The need for food and protection forced Oliver to practice the art of archery. For five years he sharpened his skills with a bow until he developed into an expert marksman.

In the first episode of *Arrow*, Oliver reminiscences, "The island held many dangers. To live, I had to make myself more than what I was, to forge myself into a weapon."[1] In the animated television series *The Batman*, Oliver recalls his time on the island, "Every day I built up my strength, tested my limits, and kept on going. I became strong, fearless."[2] Oliver used his time on the island to make himself stronger, smarter, and sharper.

Likewise, Joseph used his suffering as an opportunity to discover and develop skills that he never knew he had. After being sold on the auction block in Egypt, Joseph finds himself to be a slave in service of Pharaoh's captain of the guard, Potiphar. The Bible says,

> The LORD was with Joseph, so he succeeded in everything he did as he served in the home of his Egyptian master. Potiphar noticed this and realized that the LORD was with Joseph, giving him success in everything he did. This pleased Potiphar, so he soon made Joseph his personal attendant. He put him in charge of his entire household and everything he owned. From the day Joseph was put in charge of his master's household and property, the LORD began to bless Potiphar's household for Joseph's sake. All his household affairs ran smoothly, and his crops and livestock flourished. So Potiphar gave Joseph complete administrative responsibility over everything he owned. With Joseph there, he didn't worry about a thing—except what kind of food to eat! (Genesis 39:2-6, NLT)

In verse 1, Joseph arrived in Egypt battered and bruised. He had no possessions and no useful skills or life experience. But one thing he did have: God. The Lord loved Joseph and had a plan for his life. So God blessed Joseph's work. By the end of verse 4, Joseph is overseeing everything for the man who oversees security for

Pharaoh. Joseph utilized his time as a slave in a foreign land to learn the culture and customs of Egypt and along the way discovered a flair for management. He learned the ins and outs of authority and administration, and within a few short years, he became a master manager.

What if you and I did the same thing that Oliver and Joseph did? What if we viewed our struggles and sorrows as an opportunity to sharpen our skills or hone hidden talents? What if we used our suffering to make us stronger? In the epistle bearing his name, James urged the early Christians to do just that: "Dear brothers and sisters, when troubles of any kind come your way, consider it an opportunity for great joy. For you know that when your faith is tested, your endurance has a chance to grow. So let it grow, for when your endurance is fully developed, you will be perfect and complete, needing nothing" (James 1:2-4, NLT).

James didn't say "if" trouble comes your way, but "when" it does. He accepted that we will have problems and assured the early believers that it was possible to profit from them. His point wasn't simply to put on a happy face when difficulties or dilemmas arise, but to maintain a positive outlook, knowing that problems can produce perseverance. Mark Twain agreed. He once said, "Be careful to take from an experience only the wisdom that is in it."[3]

Joseph never read James's words, but he lived by the same principle every day (see Genesis 45:4-8). It may not be easy, but you and I ought to do the same. Take a hard look at the thing that is making you suffer and ask, "What can I learn from this? How can this experience make me stronger?"

Once you figure that out, you can bet that God will give you plenty of opportunities to use your knowledge and skills to serve others, which is exactly what Joseph and Oliver did with their now-sharpened skills.

SEASON OF SERVING

In the opening scene of *Arrow*'s pilot episode, Oliver narrates, "I am returning not the boy who was shipwrecked, but the man who will bring justice to those who have poisoned my city."[4] Once rescued and returned home, Oliver utilizes the skills that he honed on the island to become a hero, a hooded vigilante who protects the people of Starling City with a quiver full of green arrows. In the first season alone, Green Arrow stops a lethal assassin known as Deadshot, prevents a vengeful Huntress from killing her own father, thwarts a drug cartel led by Count Vertigo, and foils the plans of Malcom Merlin, a megalomaniacal mastermind bent on destroying Starling City.

Similarly, Joseph used the skills he learned as Potiphar's slave to save a nation from starvation. When Pharaoh's disturbing dreams seem to reveal a foreboding future, he turns to Joseph. Not only did Joseph foresee the famine thanks to God's intervention, but he devised a plan to survive it. He tells Pharaoh:

> Therefore, Pharaoh should find an intelligent and wise man and put him in charge of the entire land of Egypt. Then Pharaoh should appoint supervisors over the land and let them collect one-fifth of all the crops during the seven good years. Have them gather all the food produced in the good years that are just ahead and bring it to Pharaoh's storehouses. Store it away, and guard it so there will be food in the cities. That way there will be enough to eat when the seven years of famine come to the land of Egypt. Otherwise this famine will destroy the land. (Genesis 41:33-36, NLT)

Joseph's suggestions were well-received by Pharaoh and his officials. So Pharaoh said to Joseph, "Since God has revealed the meaning of the dreams to you, clearly no one else is as intelligent or wise as you are. You will be in charge of my court, and all my people will take orders from you. Only I, sitting on my throne, will have a rank higher than yours" (Genesis 41:39-40, NLT).

Joseph spent the rest of his life not only as the vice-president of Egypt, but also as a national treasure, a hero to the people. I can imagine that when Joseph stepped out on his balcony, the crowd cheered. When his chariot rolled passed, they threw flowers. The lessons that Joseph learned in the pit and the prison prepared him for the palace. Reflecting on his life in Egypt, Joseph surmises, "God sent me here...to save people's lives" (Genesis 45:5, NCV). Oliver came to a similar conclusion: "I have come home with only one goal—to save my city."[5]

Joseph and Oliver's suffering prepared them for service. Yours can do the same. When we endure painful experiences, we can allow God to use them to equip us for service to others. This might go without saying, but whatever you're going through, you're not the first person to go through it, and you won't be the last. Seventy-six percent of Americans are living paycheck to paycheck.[6] Many marriages end in divorce. Almost one million Americans filed for bankruptcy in 2014.[7] Almost three million women are treated for breast cancer every year.[8] And each year Americans take twenty-nine billion doses of aspirin (as a pain killer or as a measure to prevent heart attack).[9] Who knows how many people have experienced your same struggles? And who better to help them than you? Who better to encourage an alcoholic than a recovered alcoholic? Who better to comfort someone suffering the heartache of divorce than a fellow divorcée or divorcé? Who better to tend to a cancer victim than a cancer survivor?

God won't let your suffering go to waste. In fact, your greatest ministry will likely come out of your greatest misery. The Bible says, "God is our merciful Father and the source of all comfort. He comforts us in all our troubles so that we can comfort others. When they are troubled, we will be able to give them the same comfort God has given us" (2 Corinthians 1:3-4, NLT).

Don't let your experiences—good or bad—go to waste. Oliver Queen shared his survival skills in order to save others. When bad things happen to you, turn to God for comfort and learn what you can from your suffering. When bad things happen to others, share with them what you've learned and comfort them the way God comforts you.

***

Years later, looking back on everything that happened, Joseph assured his brothers, "You intended to harm me, but God intended it all for good" (Genesis 50:20, NLT). The story of Green Arrow, as well as the story of Joseph, underscore an important truth: in the right hands, intended evil becomes eventual good. Oliver spent five years on a hellish island. Maybe you can relate. Everyone has bad days, bad months, and even bad years. Everyone suffers. But if you'll use your season of suffering to sharpen your skills for service to others—well, it doesn't get much more heroic than that.

NOTES

1. "Pilot," *Arrow* #1 (CW Network, 2012).

2. "Vertigo," *The Batman* #55 (Kids' WB, 2007).

3. TwainQuotes.com, "Experience," http://www.twainquotes.com/Experience.html.

4. "Pilot," *Arrow* #1 (CW Network, 2012).

5. "City of Heroes," *Arrow* #24 (CW Network, 2013).

6. Angela Johnson, "76% of Americans Are Living Paycheck-to-Paycheck," *CNNMoney*, June 24, 2013, http://money.cnn.com/2013/06/24/pf/emergency-savings/index.html.

7. Debt.org, "Bankruptcy," https://www.debt.org/bankruptcy/.

8. American Cancer Society, *Breast Cancer Facts & Figures,*

2013–2014 (Atlanta: American Cancer Society, 2013), http://www.cancer.org/acs/groups/content/@research/documents/d ocument/acspc-042725.pdf.

9. Rome Neal, "World's Wonder Drug," *CBS News*, February 10, 2004, http://www.cbsnews.com/news/worlds-wonder-drug/.

14
HAWKMAN

No one loved superheroes more than Dennis, a wheelchair-bound fifty-five-year-old man with mental and physical disabilities. When a rapidly spreading cancer threatened to take Dennis's life, a group of cosplayers from Saint Louis started a project called Cards for Dennis. They invited and encouraged costumers from all over the country to send him in-character Christmas cards, hoping to give Dennis the best Christmas of his life. As the project spread through social media, Dennis was so overwhelmed with responses that Facebook banned him for exceeding the allowed limit of personal messages. Many cosplayers even came to visit Dennis in person. But even as he received hugs and handshakes from the likes of Superman, Wonder Woman, Captain America, and even Ghost Rider, Dennis always seemed to be looking over their shoulders, hoping for the appearance of his favorite superhero: Hawkman.

In the costuming community, there is one couple whose names are synonymous with Hawkman and Hawkgirl, and they are Santino and Tammy Marani. Santino and Tammy are husband and wife costumers from Benton, Kentucky. They're also committed Christians and co-creators of Costumers for Christ. While they occasionally cosplay as other comic book characters, they are renowned for their portrayal of the Hawks. When they heard about Dennis and how much he loved Hawkman, they decided to drive the four hours from Benton to Saint Louis to pay him a special visit.

Although the cancer had sapped much of his strength and stamina, Dennis's spirit soared when he saw Hawkman and Hawkgirl spread their wings at his bedside. The costumed couple kept the visit short, but they prayed with Dennis before departing and left a copy of *The Amazing Gospel*, which one of Dennis's nurses promised to read to him. Rather than making the long drive home the same day, Santino and Tammy spent the night at our home in Palmyra, Illinois. We played cards, talked ministry, and enjoyed one another's fellowship. In the morning, we got the call. Dennis had passed away during the night. His nurse told Santino, "I think he was holding on just so he could see Hawkman."

My fandom may never rival Dennis's, but I still enjoy reading Hawkman's adventures. My favorite Hawkman story is told in a three-issue, prestige-format miniseries entitled *Legend of the Hawkman*. Written by Ben Raab and illustrated by Michael Lark, this miniseries touches heavily on matters of faith.

Aliens by origin, Kartar and Shayera Hol are husband and wife crime fighters from the distant planet Thanagar. Soon after their arrival on Earth, Hawkman and Hawkgirl—as they are known to humans—face an ancient evil with connections to their home planet. When a dark entity known as Thasaro threatens to destroy both worlds, Hawkgirl invites her husband, Hawkman, to pray with her. "It would mean so much to me," she says.

Despite her plea, Kartar refuses, "Shayera, I…I can't. Prayer and religion and all that just don't hold the same meaning for me as they do for you." He continues in the next panel, "Me sitting next to you, reciting words I don't even believe. I just don't want my lack of faith to cheapen yours."[1] Throughout the adventure, Shayera's faith is juxtaposed against Kartar's lack thereof.

As I read this tale of faith and faithlessness, I couldn't help but recall the words of Isaiah: "But those who hope in the LORD will renew their strength. They will soar on wings like eagles; they will run and not grow weary, they will walk and not be faint" (Isaiah 40:31, NIV). Not only does this verse call to mind the Hawks' eagle-like wings, but also it underscores the spiritual transformation that faith brings to a person. When we place our hope and faith in the one true God, we become heirs of a threefold promise capable of empowering, elevating, and sustaining us—a promise illustrated by the story and character of Hawkman.

STRENGTH

Nearly every superhero, it seems, displays some level of super-strength, and Hawkman is no exception. Unlike other heroes, however, Hawkman derives his strength from a unique element native to his home planet, Thanagar. Embedded within Hawkman's belt and boots, this "Nth metal" possesses gravity-manipulating properties that enable its wearer to lift extraordinary weights. This allows Hawkman to stand toe to toe with otherwise much more powerful adversaries. In an issue of *Superman/Batman*, a misunderstanding actually pits Hawkman against the Man of Steel. Wearing an ornate Nth-metal gauntlet called the Claw of Horus, Hawkman slugs Superman, knocking him out of the air and careening toward the earth below. Hawkman then explains, "It draws power from the magnetic core of the earth. Essentially, I just hit you with the planet!"[2]

Similarly, God promises to supply strength to those who put their faith and hope in him. Again, Isaiah says that "the people who trust the LORD will become strong" (Isaiah 40:31, NCV). Of course, the strength that the prophet speaks of has nothing to do with bench-pressing buildings or socking supervillains. Rather, God promises to provide faithful followers with strength of spirit.

Through faith, God empowers our spirits to accomplish great things. Jesus told his followers, "I tell you the truth, if you had faith even as small as a mustard seed, you could say to this mountain, 'Move from here to there,' and it would move. Nothing would be impossible" (Matthew 17:20, NLT). In other words, a little faith can go a long way.

The eleventh chapter of the book of Hebrews overflows with the success stories of God's faithful. It recounts Abel's offering, Enoch's ascension, Abraham's travels, Jacob's and Joseph's triumphs, Moses' miracles, and much more. The common thread linking these biblical heroes together is faith. Every introduction begins with faith: by faith Abel brought an offering; by faith Enoch walked with God; by faith Noah built an ark; by faith Abraham obeyed God's call; by faith Sarah conceived; by faith Moses led the people; by faith Rahab was not destroyed—and the list goes on. Each of these great men and women accomplished incredible feats for God, and they did it all by faith. Toward the end of the chapter, God tells us that through faith, "Their weakness was turned to strength. They became strong in battle and put whole armies to flight" (Hebrews 11:34, NLT). Wouldn't you like your weakness to be turned to strength?

This is God's promise to those who live by faith. You'll find yourself able to do things by faith that you never thought you could do. Who would have imagined Hawkman knocking out the Man of Steel? Just as Hawkman enjoys enhanced strength when he puts on his Nth-metal garments, Christians experience a heightened strength of spirit when we put on Christ. The apostle Paul put it this way: "For I can do everything through Christ, who gives me strength" (Philippians 4:13, NLT).

Whatever challenges we meet, whatever obstacles we encounter, as long as our faith rests firmly in the Lord, Christ will give us the strength we need to face them. But strength isn't the only promise that God gives those who hope in him. He also offers the promise of soaring, which is another ability possessed by Hawkman.

SOARING

What comic book buff hasn't closed his or her eyes and imagined soaring through the sky? The power of flight is fairly common among comic book characters, but few superheroes take to the skies as naturally as Hawkman. Just as with his enhanced strength, Hawkman derives his flying ability from the gravity-defying Nth metal grafted into his armor. Rather than being a part of Hawkman's anatomy, his massive wings connect to a harness and respond to the subtle movement of his shoulders.

It is these majestic wings that make Hawkman such a rare and difficult character to cosplay. Few costumers are able to concoct a method of building them that doesn't cost a fortune. Santino and Tammy developed a technique involving headliner foam, PVC pipes, and pulleys. This simple system allows them to pull a string and suddenly unfurl their feathers—a trick that impresses the judges at every costume contest they enter. No matter how impressive they are to see, however, their wings will never enable them to get off the ground.

God, on the other hand, tells us that "those who trust in the LORD will…soar on wings like eagles" (Isaiah 40:31, NIV). As with the promise of strength, the promise of soaring has little to do with literal flying. Rather, this imagery of rising up on eagles' wings points to an ability to rise above earthly concerns and draw near to the God who inhabits the heavens. The same imagery appears earlier in the Bible after God rescued the people of Israel from slavery in Egypt. The Lord assured them, "You have seen what I did to the Egyptians. You know how I carried you on eagles' wings and brought you to myself" (Exodus 19:4, NLT). Again, rising up on eagles' wings parallels being brought near to God. In other words, faith enables us to reach unimaginable spiritual heights, and the higher we soar, the closer we come to God. Through faith we draw near to God, experience God's presence, and enjoy communion with the Lord.

To people such as Abraham, Sarah, and other heroes of the Bible, God wasn't just an idea adopted by the mind, but rather an experiential reality that gave meaning to their lives. Only through faith we can draw near to God in the same way. Just as Hawkman's Nth-metal wings enable him to soar through the heavens, the wings of faith empower us to soar into the transcendent presence of the God of heaven.

Scripture says, "And without faith it is impossible to please him, for whoever would draw near to God must believe that he exists and that he rewards those who seek him" (Hebrews 11:6, ESV). If you reach out to the Lord in faith, God will be revealed to you personally. In fact, the Bible invites, "Let us come near to God with a sincere heart and a sure faith" (Hebrews 10:22, NCV). It's hard to imagine a feeling more euphoric than soaring though the skies free and unfettered, yet an encounter with the living God can elevate our spirits higher than any eagle (or hawk) can fly.

This nearness and intimacy with God generates confidence, courage, and comfort in the life of a believer. It raises our spirits, provides us with a blessed assurance, and produces a peace that surpasses all understanding.

STAMINA

Every superhero needs stamina, not just when facing supervillains, but even more importantly, when facing dwindling sales! Countless comic book titles have faced cancellation over the years, causing many of the starring characters to fade into obscurity. The same could easily have been true of Hawkman. He first appeared in *Flash Comics* #1 in 1940, and enjoyed a recurring role in that series throughout the following decade. Along with many other superheroes, however, Hawkman's Golden Age adventures came to an end when the comics industry stumbled in the early 1950s. He last appeared in *All Star Comics* #57 in 1951.

Hawkman refused to go quietly into the night though. Ten years later, DC Comics editor Julius Schwartz reinvented and reintroduced the character in *The Brave and the Bold* #34. Fans adored the new version of Hawkman, and he earned his own title in 1964. Unfortunately, it lasted just twenty-seven issues before being cancelled. In the 1980s DC tested the waters with a Hawkman miniseries that revived interest in the character and led to another ongoing series, but again the series faced cancellation after only seventeen issues. Since then, Hawkman has starred in three more titles, each one cancelled after only two or three years. But despite poor sales and repeated cancellations, Hawkman remains one of DCs most iconic and enduring superheroes. Dedicated fans will finally see Hawkman take flight in a live action television series in the CW Network's *Legends of Tomorrow*. Hawkman's faithful fans have kept him going for more than seventy years.

What keeps you going?

Christians may not have to worry about our comic book being cancelled, but we do face our own challenges. Are you discouraged as a parent? Are you pessimistic about your job? Ready to give up on your marriage? Or the hope of ever getting married? Are you weary with doing good? Can't resist temptation? Is your day framed with sorrow and disappointment? Are your tomorrows turning into never? Is *hope* a forgotten word?

Have you grown weary and tired? Feel like throwing in the towel? Then listen once more to the words of Isaiah: "Those who trust in the LORD ... will run and not grow weary. They will walk and not faint" (Isaiah 40:31, NLT).

Faith keeps you going.

Even before trusting in the divine, Hawkman recognized the power of faith. At a critical point in the story, Hawkman's demonic nemesis Thasaro boasts, "Nothing can destroy me! Not the weapons of man! Not the gods! Least of all, a faithless little gnat who believes in nothing." Hawkman responds, "I believe in courage. I believe in friendship. I believe in love. That is my faith. That is what gives me power. And that is your doom!"[3]

No matter what struggles or obstacles we face, faith can sustain us. In fact, the New Testament urges, "Dear brothers and sisters, when troubles of any kind come your way, consider it an opportunity for great joy. For you know that when your faith is tested, your endurance has a chance to grow" (James 1:2-3, NLT). As we learned from Green Arrow, facing trials and troubles isn't a matter of *if*, but *when*. God knows that you'll have difficulties that test your faith, but the Lord won't leave you alone with your problems. God's Spirit stays close and helps you grow.

Are you close to quitting? Don't do it. Hang on to the hand of God, and hang in there.

***

In the final chapter of *Legend of the Hawkman*, Shayera suffers a grave injury to her abdomen. Although she survives, her Thanagarian doctors inform her that she will never be able to bear children. Driven by compassion for his heartbroken wife, Kartar decides to give faith a chance. He finds an ancient cathedral, where he finally kneels in prayer. There he receives a heavenly vision and the promise that his beautiful bride will be healed.

After Kartar finally vanquishes his fearsome foe, the story concludes in a Christian church on the Earth, where Hawkman and Hawkgirl are ordained as godparents of a police friend's newborn. During the ceremony, the officiant asks, "Wilt thou obediently keep God's holy will and his commandments, and walk in the same all the days of thy life?" Together, the winged couple responds, "I will." Following the ceremony, Hawkgirl looks lovingly into her husband's eyes and inquires, "What about us, Kartar? Will we ever be so blessed?" Stretching out his magnificent wings, Kartar takes his wife by the hand, and the two of them rise into the clear blue sky, as Kartar smiles and says, "Shayera, honey…I have it on good faith."[4]

In the end, Hawkman discovered the value of faith and committed himself to walking in the will and the Word of God. If you'll do the same, then you too will discover renewed strength, stamina, and the ability to soar on the wings of faith.

NOTES

1. Ben Raab (writer) and Michael Lark (artist), "Heresy," *Legend of the Hawkman* #2 (DC Comics, 2000).

2. Jeph Loeb (writer) and Ed McGuiness (artist), *Superman/ Batman* #4 (DC Comics, 2004).

3. Ben Raab (writer) and Michael Lark (artist), "Flight of Faith," *Legend of the Hawkman* #3 (DC Comics, 2000).

4. Ibid.

15
CYBORG

I first met John Clark at one of the many comic book conventions that Ashley and I attend. John was a vender selling original artwork as well as cosplay props such as helmets, hammers, and other hardware. When John learned about Costumers for Christ and our mission to share Christ through comics and cosplay, he volunteered to take some of our comics and outreach pamphlets and display them on his table at the many conventions that he travels to. Thanks to John, the gospel continues to spread throughout the geek community. Among John's many comics-inspired costumes, perhaps the most iconic is his portrayal of DC's mechanical man, Cyborg.

Though lesser-known to mainstream audiences, Cyborg remains a fan favorite of comic collectors and is rumored to make his cinematic debut in the feature film *Batman v. Superman: Dawn of Justice*, due for release in March of 2016. After a nearly fatal accident, Victor Stone was cybernetically enhanced by his father. Now a capable crime fighter and successful superhero, Victor possesses augmented strength and the ability to communicate, manipulate, and interface with nearly all forms of technology. But perhaps Cyborg's greatest power is his ability to overcome the many obstacles and challenges that life throws at him.

Hardships and adversity permeate Victor's life, many of which stem from the disfiguring accident that ultimately transformed him into Cyborg. Yet, time and again, Victor manages to overcome. As Christians, we can learn a lot from Cyborg about overcoming the challenges that we face. In surveying Cyborg's story, I see three obstacles that stand out, each of which is common to people from every walk of life.

OVERCOMING INFLUENCES

Late one night, at just eight years old, Victor snuck out of his parents' house to explore the city. Unfamiliar with his surroundings, he wandered into a busy street. Horns blared. Drivers shouted. But Victor just froze in his tracks. Without a second to spare, a teenage boy dove at Victor, shoving him to safety. The boy introduced himself as Ron Evers. And that's how Victor met his first friend.

To a sheltered, withdrawn kid like Victor, Ron seemed streetwise and exciting. Victor begins following in Ron's footsteps. Despite his introductory act of heroism, however, Ron leads Victor down a troubled path. When the two of them are arrested for looting a grocery store, Victor's dad expresses disappointment in his son: "Look what associating with others has already done, Victor. You're a hooligan."[1] Not long after, Ron gets Victor involved in a gang fight that lands Victor in the hospital and Ron in jail.

Temporarily separated from Ron's influence, Victor enjoys more positive pursuits: attending high school, excelling in sports, and dating. Years later, released from prison, Ron tries to convince Victor to join a small terrorist cell intent on blowing up S.T.A.R. Labs. Victor, now a marriage of man and machine, shows up at the appointed time and place atop the facility. But to Ron's surprise, Victor announces, "You're not going to take out the lab. I'm not here to help you, Ron. I'm here to stop you."[2] Hoisting the now-hardened and hate-filled criminal above his head, Victor declares, "You're bad news, Ron. You always were."[3]

By overcoming Ron's negative influence, Victor saved the day and became a hero. Of course, Victor isn't the only one who wrestles with negative influences. The Bible warns us about the company we keep: "Happy are those who don't listen to the wicked, who don't go where sinners go, who don't do what evil people do" (Psalm 1:1, NCV). In other words, it's important for us to separate ourselves from negative, even evil, influences. The Bible also warns, "Do not be deceived: 'Bad company corrupts good morals'" (1 Corinthians 15:33, ESV). Victor was led down a dangerous and potentially deadly path because of the company he kept. The same can happen to us.

Now, this doesn't mean that we shouldn't have any association with people who are not Christians. That's not the point. Jesus often hung out with nonreligious types—people whom "decent" folks avoided—but Jesus wasn't there just to have a good time and go along with the crowd. Rather, he was there to be a light in the darkness.

That's eventually what Victor became. Even as they battled upon the roof of S.T.A.R. Labs, bullets bouncing off of Victor's cybernetic skin, Victor never stopped caring for his friend. He tried reasoning with Ron. "There's got to be a better way," Victor pleaded. Recalling the events of that night later, Victor reflected, "I thought I could save the city and my former best friend."[4] Sadly, Victor learned a painful lesson: we can't save everybody. Cyborg later tells his teammates that Ron was "killed by his own hate."[5] Scripture says it clearly: "the path of the wicked leads to destruction" (Psalm 1:6, NLT).

Like Victor, we might need to take a hard look at our relationships. Like it or not, we are constantly influencing the people around us, and the people around us are constantly influencing us. So, are the people in your life influencing you in a good and godly way? Or are they influencing you in a harmful and hateful way? We need to be wise about the company we keep and the influences we allow into our lives.

OVERCOMING ISOLATION

While Victor was visiting his mother and father's laboratory at S.T.A.R. Labs, an extradimensional experiment gone wrong resulted in an explosion. Victor's mom, Elinore Stone, died in the blast, and Victor's own body was ripped apart. Silas Stone, Victor's father, used experimental cybernetic parts developed for the military to save his son, rebuilding the teenager's broken body piece by piece. Bone was replaced with steel, and flesh with special polymers. Veins and arteries were encased in plastic tubing, and metal straps bound it all together. When Victor awoke in his cybernetic body, his half-human appearance horrified him.

Victor's first instinct certainly wasn't to become a superhero; he simply sought a normal life. He wanted to go back to school, play football, and be accepted. But when Victor attempted to reenter the world, he experienced nothing but fear and revulsion in those around him. "I felt their eyes boring into me," Cyborg recalls. "Fear. Hate. It hurt so much. I was a monster. A blasted Frankenstein."[6] He tried to reconnect with his girlfriend, Marcy, but she stopped retuning his calls. At school, Victor was banned from playing football because of his cybernetic enhancements. When the coach caught Victor training by himself on the football field, he said, "Please, Victor. Don't do this to yourself. You don't belong here anymore." Victor snapped back, "Then where in blazes do I belong?"[7]

All of us need a place to belong, don't we? Sadly, too many people can relate to Cyborg's situation. Maybe you know what it's like to look different and to be treated differently. Perhaps you've felt the sting of rejection. What is often worse is that, like Victor, the more rejection we experience, the more withdrawn and isolated we become. Stephen Ilardi, writing for *Psychology Today*, calls social isolation "a modern plague," noting that "25% of Americans have no meaningful social support at all—not a single person they can confide in." This isolation takes its toll, making us more vulnerable to mental illness, depression, and addiction.[8]

Thankfully, Victor found a place to belong. Shortly after his rooftop heroics, an eminent threat prompted a mysterious superhero, Raven, to form a new team, called the Teen Titans. She first recruits experienced sidekicks, including Robin, Wonder Girl, and Kid Flash, among others. Then, in a puff of purple smoke, she appears to Cyborg, and says, "You belong with me, Victor Stone, with others of your kind." Surrounded by the likes of Beast Boy, a green-skinned shape-shifter, and Starfire, an orange alien, Cyborg responds, "A freak among freaks, right?"[9]

Although apprehensive at first, Victor found a place among the Titans where he was accepted and appreciated, regardless of his inhuman appearance. "The Titans gave me the family my parents never could," Cyborg reminisces. "They didn't look at me as a freak."[10]

The church could learn a lot from the Teen Titans. The Bible urges us, "Accept each other just as Christ has accepted you" (Romans 15:7, NLT). We learned from Batman and the Fantastic Four that the church is meant to be a family, but in order to be that family, we must create a place of openness and acceptance. Just as Raven did for Cyborg, we need to reach out to the outcasts, the ones who feel like freaks, and those whom society pushes to its fringes, and let them know that they aren't alone. Neither appearance, age, ethnicity, sexual orientation, income level, nor anything else should prevent the church from reaching out to someone and saying, "You belong with us." Cyborg overcame his isolation only with the help of the Titans. With the help of Christ's church, we can do the same.

OVERCOMING INABILITIES

In an episode of the animated series *Teen Titans*, Cyborg works out with his teammates. Robin strikes at a wing chun dummy. Starfire blasts automated, airborne droids. Beast Boy tests his speed as a cheetah on a treadmill. And Cyborg grimaces beneath a monstrous amount of weight. As the hydraulic machine increase the weight, a digital readout on Cyborg's arm monitors his power output. "Come on, Cyborg, push," Robin prods his teammate. Beast Boy chimes in, "Punch it, Cy! Straight through the roof."

When Cyborg's power output reaches 100 percent, he grunts, "It's no good. Shut it down." But Robin pushes him onward, "No way, Cyborg. I won't let you quit!" "I can't," Cyborg warns. "Yes, you can," Robin calls back. Finally, Cyborg dives out from under the mammoth machine, a split second before being crushed beneath it.

"I was just trying to get you to kick it up a notch," Robin explains apologetically. "I don't have another notch," Cyborg snaps. "I'm not like you, okay. When I say I can't, I can't. When I was an athlete...when I was human...I loved pushing my limits, getting stronger, faster, better—just by trying harder than I ever had before. My coaches always told me to give 110 percent and I always did. But my muscles are mechanical now. Limits are built in. No matter how hard I try, 100 percent is all I've got." Cyborg spends the rest of the day wallowing in his feelings of failure.

Eventually, his limits are put to the test when an atrocious android named Atlas captures his teammates and challenges Cyborg to one-on-one combat. Atlas is inarguably the stronger and faster of the two. As their battle reaches its climax, Cyborg's power output once again reaches 100 percent. Convinced of his own limitations, Cyborg gives up and retreats.[11]

Many of us struggle with our own inabilities and limitations, some of them self-imposed. Maybe you have a physical weakness or handicap. Maybe you're socially awkward or you have a learning disability. Maybe you have a relationship that seems impossible to repair or bills that seem impossible to pay. Moses felt limited by his inability to speak. Gideon felt limited by the size of his army. Rachel felt limited by her inability to conceive children. Naomi felt limited by her grief. The disciples felt limited by a basket of only five loaves and two fish. Our limitations can either defeat us or challenge us to overcome them.

Realizing that his friends need him, Cyborg returns later in the episode for a rematch with Atlas. Once again the pitched battle reaches its climax, and Cyborg's power output reaches 100 percent. But this time, Cyborg doesn't give up. With his teammates cheering him on, Cyborg pushes himself beyond his limitations. His digital readout climbs to 110 percent, then 120, and then 130. Cyborg overpowers his enemy and saves his friends.

Through faith and perseverance Cyborg overcame his limitations. We can too. When your situation seems impossible, remember the words of Jesus: "Humanly speaking, it is impossible. But not with God. Everything is possible with God" (Mark 10:27, NLT). When we believe in God and believe in ourselves, we'll find that we're capable of far more than we ever imagined.

* * *

Cyborg stands as a powerful example for both committed Christians and spiritual seekers. His conscience and strength of character allowed him to overcome sinister influences. His desire to belong enabled him to overcome social isolation. And his perseverance and determination empowered him to overcome seeming inabilities. Like Victor, we all face obstacles and challenges. But, like him, we too can overcome. The Bible reassures us, "Despite all these things, overwhelming victory is ours through Christ, who loved us" (Romans 8:37, NLT).

NOTES

1. Marv Wolfman (writer) and George Pérez (artist), "Cyborg," *The New Teen Titans* #1 (DC Comics, 1980).

2. Mark Sable (writer) and Ken Lashley (artist), *Cyborg* #1 (DC Comics, 2008).

3. Marv Wolfman (writer) and George Pérez (artist), "Cyborg," *The New Teen Titans* #1 (DC Comics, 1980).

4. Mark Sable (writer) and Ken Lashley (artist), *Cyborg* #1 (DC Comics, 2008).

5. Marv Wolfman (writer) and George Pérez (artist), "Cyborg," *The New Teen Titans* #1 (DC Comics, 1980).

6. Ibid.

7. Marv Wolfman (writer) and George Pérez (artist), "Cyborg," *The New Teen Titans* #1 (DC Comics, 1980).

8. Stephen Ilardi, "Social Isolation: A Modern Plague," *Psychology Today*, July 13, 2009, https://www.psychologytoday.com/blog/the-depression-cure/200907/social-isolation-modern-plague.

9. Marv Wolfman (writer) and George Pérez (artist), "Cyborg," *The New Teen Titans* #1 (DC Comics, 1980).

10. Mark Sable (writer) and Ken Lashley (artist), *Cyborg* #1 (DC Comics, 2008).

11. "Only Human," *Teen Titans* #17 (Cartoon Network, 2004).

16
THOR

Shortly after creating the Hulk, Stan Lee felt it necessary to devise a powerful force for good strong enough to defeat the giant green rage-monster should the need arise. His solution: the Mighty Thor. Based on the legends of Norse mythology, Thor holds the title of Marvel's mightiest Avenger.

While I've yet to cosplay as Thor myself, the son of Odin remains one of my son's recurring characters. Yeshua first cosplayed as the mightiest Avenger in 2009, at the age of four! Along with several costuming friends, our family cosplayed the entire Avengers lineup in Metropolis. Together we entered the costume contest on the last day of the Superman Celebration. While each of our Avengers looked outstanding, my son's miniature Thor won us first place in our category and third overall.

During the contest, each of us walked to the front of the stage and back again, allowing the judges to get a close look at our costumes. As Yeshua reached the edge of the platform, he thrust his hammer into the air and shouted, "For Odin and for Asgard!" The crowd went crazy and Yeshua just soaked up the applause. My wife literally had to drag him off the stage, which was just all the more entertaining for the audience. Since then, Yeshua's enthusiasm and extroverted personality have made him an asset to our costuming ministry. He regularly reprises the role of Thor at comic conventions, charity events, and other costuming occasions.

As the son of a mythological god, Thor bears some resemblance to Jesus; however, he lacks many of the character traits necessary to make him a compelling Christ-figure. Rather, despite his godlike power, Thor actually holds more in common with you and me. In Marvel's 2011 film, Thor is portrayed as a brash, headstrong prince set to inherit the throne from his father, Odin. He relishes adventure and craves battle. Driven by selfishness and pride, Thor breaks a truce between the Asgardians and their enemies, the brutal Frost Giants, nearly starting a war. In order to teach his son a lesson in humility, Odin strips Thor of his power and mighty hammer and banishes him to a distant land—Earth. Humbled and humiliated in an unfamiliar realm, Thor eventually comes to his senses, repents of his foolish ways, and learns the value of selflessness. In the end, Thor foils the evil plots of his jealous brother, Loki, and reunites with his father, who welcomes him to the realm eternal.[1]

The story of Thor, albeit fictional and fantastic, at its core greatly resembles a parable Jesus once told—another fictional story about a wayward son and loving father. We call it the parable of the prodigal son. Like Thor's story, the prodigal is a tale about a father's all-encompassing, incomprehensible love. And both stories illustrate the stages that we often go through in our own parent-child relationships, whether as a Norse god on Asgard, as humans on Earth, or as humans with our Heavenly Father. The first of those stages is rebellion.

REBELLION

Both Thor and the prodigal son rebelled against their respective fathers. Thor defied Odin's orders, endangering the lives of everyone on Asgard. The prodigal's rebellion was more subtle, but probably even more hurtful. Jesus tells it this way: "A man had two sons. The younger son told his father, 'I want my share of your estate now before you die.' So his father agreed to divide his wealth between his sons. A few days later this younger son packed all his belongings and moved to a distant land, and there he wasted all his money in wild living" (Luke 15:11-13, NLT).

In ancient times, the younger son normally would inherit half as much as the firstborn son (so, about a third of the estate in this case) when their father died. It wasn't completely unheard of to ask for your portion of the inheritance while your father still lived, but it certainly wasn't very loving either. It showed the younger son's arrogance and disrespect for his father. It was as if he had said to his dad, "I wish you were already dead!"

Both Thor and the prodigal grew up in their father's home, they were showered with love, they had everything they needed, and a lavish inheritance awaited them, but the prodigal son grew weary of living under his father's roof and following his father's rules. He wanted to be his own man—to do things his way—and it didn't matter whom he hurt in the process.

Maybe you can relate. We all possess a rebellious streak. The Bible calls it our "sinful nature," and it means that we have a natural inclination to put ourselves first, to rebel not only against our parents, but even against our Heavenly Father. An old hymn written by Robert Robinson expresses it eloquently: "Prone to wander, Lord, I feel it, prone to leave the God I love."

Today 320 million people live in the United States, and as many as 80 percent of them identify themselves as Christians, yet a study by Lifeway Research reveals that only 20 percent actually attend church from week to week.[2] If I understand these statistics correctly, many Americans still think of themselves as a part of God's family, but they haven't set foot in their Heavenly Father's house for who knows how long. This suggests that many of them are prodigal children—once-faithful followers of Jesus who have wandered from home and left the God they loved.

Perhaps you're a prodigal yourself. Maybe you once had a vibrant faith and were active in some local church, but something happened. Maybe you relocated after college or marriage or retirement, and you never got around to finding a new church home. Maybe life's transitions—such as a full-time job or parenting or chronic illness—caused you to fall out of the habit of regular attendance. Perhaps you suffered a deep loss, and you just can't believe a loving God would allow such pain. Maybe you've been hurt by a judgmental pastor or a church member's betrayal. Whatever caused you to wander away, there comes a time when you realize how long it's been since you said a prayer or sat in a pew. You realize how far you've wandered from the God who loves you.

That's where both Thor and the prodigal son found themselves. Thankfully, that's also where they both came to their senses. The second stage in their relationship with their respective fathers was repentance.

REPENTANCE

In a dramatic scene in the 2011 film, Thor came to a sobering realization. Even after being cast out of Asgard, Thor assumed that once he found his magical hammer, Mjölnir, his power and glory would be restored to him. Unbeknownst to Thor, however, Odin placed an enchantment on the hammer, whispering the words, "Whosoever holds this hammer, if he be worthy, shall possess the power of Thor." After an arduous search and hard-fought battle, Thor finally finds his hammer in a S.H.I.E.L.D. compound. But as he wraps his fingers tightly around its handle, he discovers that he can't lift it. His muscles strain and his teeth grind, but no matter how hard he tries, he can't budge the hammer. He's no longer worthy. When he could no longer wield his own hammer, Thor finally realized how unworthy he had become.

Far from home, away from the guidance and wisdom of his father, the prodigal son came to a similar recognition. He wasted all of his inheritance on wild living, and it was then, Jesus said, that "a great famine swept over the land, and he began to starve. He persuaded a local farmer to hire him, and the man sent him into his fields to feed the pigs. The young man became so hungry that even the pods he was feeding the pigs looked good to him. But no one gave him anything" (Luke 15:14-16, NLT).

My mom often said that my bedroom looked like a pigpen. Well, this boy's room actually was one. While the hogs he tended wallowed in the mud, the prodigal wallowed in his own misery and self-loathing. As he lay there surrounded by unclean animals, his mind kept drifting back home—to his father's house. He thought to himself, "All those farmhands working for my father sit down to three meals a day, and here I am starving to death" (Luke 15:17, MSG).

This starving young man knew that his wealthy father would not fall asleep without dinner that night. Even the farmhands on his father's land had plenty of food and a roof over their heads. But not him. Friendless and foodless, this boy had hit rock bottom, and that, the Bible says, is when "he finally came to his senses" (Luke 15:17, TLB). He decided to go to his father and tell him, "I am no longer worthy of being called your son" (Luke 15:19, NLT).

Thor and the prodigal are not the only unworthy ones. The truth is, we're all unworthy. Not one of us is worthy to be called a child of God. The Bible says, "There is no difference; for all have sinned and fall short of the glory of God" (Romans 3:22-23, NJKV). For many of us, it takes hitting rock bottom to realize how truly wrong we've been and how far we've fallen. But recognizing our faults and failures isn't enough if we don't do something about it.

An old *Peanuts* cartoon strip opens with Lucy holding a football and inviting Charlie Brown to kick it, but Charlie Brown refuses. He says, "Every time I try to kick the ball, you move it and I fall flat on my back." Suddenly, Lucy breaks down in tears and confesses, "Charlie Brown, I have been so terrible to you over the years, picking up the football like that. I played so many cruel tricks on you, but I've seen the error of my ways! I've been so wrong. Won't you give a poor penitent girl another chance?" Lucy's sincerity touches Charlie Brown, who replies, "Of course I'll give you another chance." Lucy positions the ball, and Charlie runs to kick it. But at the last moment, Lucy picks up the ball, and Charlie Brown falls flat on his back, just like always. Lucy's last words are, "Recognizing your faults and actually changing your ways are two different things, Charlie Brown!"[3]

Lucy's right. The realization that we're not worthy—that we've made mistakes and that we need forgiveness—isn't enough if it doesn't drive us to get up and go back home. That's what repentance means. *Repentance* isn't just some made-up religious word. It actually comes from an essentially nomadic culture that lived in a world with no maps or street signs or GPS. It's easy to get lost walking through the desert. At some point you become aware that the countryside is strange and you're not where you should be. You finally say to yourself, *I'm going in the wrong direction*, and then you turn and go a new way. That's repentance. And that's what both Thor and the prodigal did, and as a result they finally experienced restoration.

RESTORATION

Thor's story had a happy ending, of course. After Thor sacrifices himself in battle against a twelve-foot-tall armored monstrosity from Asgard to save a small southwestern town, his power and position are restored to him. He returns to majestic Asgard just in time to rescue the throne from his mischievous brother, Loki. Odin then throws a joyful feast in Thor's honor. Overlooking the splendid spires of Asgard, Odin assures Thor, "You'll be a wise king."

Humbly, Thor replies, "There will never be a wiser king than you, nor a better father. Someday, I shall make you proud." Turning to his beloved son and placing a mighty hand upon his shoulder, Odin smiles, "You've already made be proud."[4]

The prodigal son experienced a similar homecoming: "So he returned home to his father. And while he was still a long way off, his father saw him coming. Filled with love and compassion, he ran to his son, embraced him, and kissed him" (Luke 15:20, NLT).

As the wayfaring young man comes over the hillside and catches his father's eye, he has no idea what awaits him. At best, he hopes for a cold shoulder or a disappointed lecture from his father and a haughty "I told you so" from his jealous brother. But when the father glimpses him coming over the horizon, the older man rushes to his long-lost son, throwing his arms around him.

With his lost son back in his loving arms, the father called for "the finest robe in the house and put it on him," symbolizing his acceptance by the family. The prodigal received "a ring for his finger and sandals for his feet." The cooks killed the fattened calf, and the celebration began. When the older son, who stayed at home by his father's side all along, expresses his jealousy, the father wisely counsels him, "My son, you are always with me, and everything I have is yours. But we had to celebrate and be glad, because this brother of yours was dead and is alive again; he was lost and is found" (Luke 15:31-32, NIV).

Of course, the father in each story points to our loving Father in heaven—standing at the edge of eternity, watching, longing for his children to come home. The Bible says, "All of us used to live that way, following the passionate desires and inclinations of our sinful nature. By our very nature we were subject to God's anger, just like everyone else. But God is so rich in mercy, and he loved us so much, that even though we were dead because of our sins, he gave us life when he raised Christ from the dead. (It is only by God's grace that you have been saved!)" (Ephesians 2:3-5, NLT).

Maybe you have wondered, when you're alone at night with just your thoughts, *Could God really forgive me? I've made so many mistakes.* I think that Jesus told this story to answer that question. No matter who we are, where we've been, or how far we've wandered, we have a Father in heaven who loves us and longs to hold us in his arms, forgive our mistakes, and give us a home with him for all eternity. To use Thor's words, "There will never be a better father."

✱✱✱

The story of Thor, along with the parable of the prodigal son, illustrates our own rebellious nature and need for repentance as well as the unrelenting love of God, our Father in heaven. Maybe you've been wrestling with a rebellious spirit. Maybe you grew up in the church, your Father's house, but for whatever reason you packed your bags and headed for a distant land far away from God. I want to encourage you to follow in Thor's footsteps, repent of your rebellious attitude, and return home to the One who loves you and is waiting for you with open arms.

NOTES
1. *Thor*, directed by Kenneth Branagh (Paramount Pictures, 2011).
2. National Back to Church Sunday, "Statistics and Research Provided by LifeWay Research," September 18, 2015, http://back-tochurch.com/participate/resources/statistics.
3. ThePreachersWord, "Admission of Wrong or Change of Heart?" January 26, 2013, http://thepreachersword.com/2013/01/26/admission-of-wrong-or-change-of-heart/.
4. *Thor*, directed by Kenneth Branagh (Paramount Pictures, 2011).

17
WONDER WOMAN

I have a special ringtone for my wife. Every time she calls me, the 1970s *Wonder Woman* television theme song resonates from my cell phone, and a smile stretches across my face. Ashley cosplays the Amazon Princess so often and so well that it's hard for me not to think of her as Wonder Woman. Even as I type this chapter, an iconic image of Ashley as Wonder Woman wallpapers my computer screen. Most recently, she cosplayed as the Amazon Princess in order to team up with our local Walmart to raise money for Children's Miracle Network. Together with some members of our church, each one donning different heroic attire, Ashley greeted customers, posed for pictures, and solicited donations to provide critical treatments and charitable care for kids in our community.

Even before Ashley cosplayed her character, though, Wonder Woman was my favorite female superhero. I recently introduced my son to the *Wonder Woman* television series starring Lynda Carter. Yeshua watches it with same wide-eyed enjoyment that I did at his age. Lynda Carter's beauty and quiet grace led to a memorable portrayal that cemented Wonder Woman's place as the greatest female superhero. More than thirty years since the series ended, her legendary status remains unchallenged. Although both the Marvel and DC universes overflow with female heroines—Storm, Electra, Scarlet Witch, Black Widow, Supergirl, Powergirl, and Batgirl, just to name a few—none of them hold a candle to Wonder Woman's iconic status. The full package of beauty, brains, and brawn, she has been admired around the world since her star-spangled debut in 1941.

In addition to being a strong female role model for young women, Wonder Woman mirrors the Christian life for men and women alike in multiple ways. Perhaps the most striking parallel is her role as an ambassador for her people.

Born Princess Diana, Wonder Woman grew up on the mystical island of Themyscira, home to a proud, strong race of warrior women known as Amazons. Her mother, Hippolyta, rules the tribe of Amazons as their queen. For centuries their utopian civilization, also known as Paradise Island, lay hidden in a vast ocean, shielded from the corrupt world of men (and in this context, it really was understood as a gender-exclusive "man's world"). But when cocky American fighter pilot Steve Trevor crash lands on the island, Queen Hippolyta decides that the time has come to rejoin the world of men and share the beauty of the Amazon culture. She holds a contest to decide which warrior will be their representative. The gladiatorial-type challenges—including a javelin toss, archery, and chariot races—test the Amazon women's strength and skill, culminating in a competition known as "bullets and bracelets," where Amazon archers take aim while contestants attempt to block the flying arrows with metal gauntlets. When Diana emerges victorious, she receives the title of Wonder Woman and travels into the human world to represent her people. Wonder Woman becomes not only an American hero, but also an emissary of the Amazons, holding diplomatic status in the United States and in the United Nations.

Just as Wonder Woman acts as ambassador of the Amazons, Christians are called to be ambassadors of Christ. In the Bible, the apostle Paul wrote this to the Christians living in his day:

All of this is a gift from God, who brought us back to himself through Christ. And God has given us this task of reconciling people to him. For God was in Christ, reconciling the world to himself, no longer counting people's sins against them. And he gave us this wonderful message of reconciliation. So we are Christ's ambassadors; God is making his appeal through us. We speak for Christ when we plead, "Come back to God!" For God made Christ, who never sinned, to be the offering for our sin, so that we could be made right with God through Christ. (2 Corinthians 5:18-21, NLT)

Being an ambassador is a huge and heavy responsibility, and not one to be taken lightly, whether you are representing the race of Amazons or the reign of God. The story of Wonder Woman offers striking parallels to the job description outlined by Paul, illustrating the ambassador's mission, message, and motivation.

OUR MISSION

In DC's original animated movie *Wonder Woman*, Queen Hippolyta commissions her daughter Diana on the scenic shores of their island paradise, "This is your mission. You, my daughter, will serve as our ambassador."[1] Hippolyta appoints Diana to become their ambassador because Diana is the best representative of her people. She embodies the virtues and qualities that Amazons treasure: strength, wisdom, compassion, and a warrior's spirit.

That's what an ambassador is—a representative. You and I didn't have to vie in a competition of bullets and bracelets to become representatives of Christ; rather, Jesus calls all of his people to be ambassadors on his behalf. Therefore, it's important for us to represent Jesus to the world by being as Christ-like as possible. As has been said, "Christians are to *be* good news before they *share* the good news."

People who don't know Jesus are constantly judging him by his followers. Few things can repel a spiritual seeker as efficiently as Christians whose character doesn't match their creed. Jesus had a word for people like that. Over and over throughout the gospels, he called them hypocrites. The word *hypocrite* actually comes from the Greek theater; *hypocrite* was the Greek word for actors who wore masks and performed on stage. Sadly, that's how much of the world sees Christians. According to a study conducted by LifeWay Research, 72 percent of people surveyed believe that churches are "full of hypocrites."[2]

If you are a Christian, you ought to know that your neighbors and co-workers have their "hypocrisy radar" constantly scanning your life. What are they picking up from you? If they detect false piety, a holier-than-thou attitude, or a spiritual stage show, then you aren't representing Jesus very well. As an ambassador for Jesus, your life should be a reflection of his life. When we lived in Saint Louis, our senior pastor often said, "We need to be Jesus to people." When we treat people the way Jesus treated people and love people the way Jesus loved people, then those people will start to see Jesus in us.

In a story written by William Messner-Loebs in the 1990s, Diana discovers a second tribe of Amazons living on Themyscira, separated centuries ago from the main tribe after Heracles and his army invaded the island. This splinter group's only connection to their past is a three-thousand-year-old sculpture of Queen Hippolyta's sister, Antiope. Yet when Diana enters their ramshackle village, she is immediately recognized as the Princess of Themyscira because of her uncanny resemblance to the sculpture.[3] Christians likewise should bear an uncanny resemblance to Jesus. No one knows what Jesus *looks* like, but the whole world should know what Jesus *is* like by the character of his ambassadors.

OUR MESSAGE

In their ancient past, the Amazon women lived among men until the demigod Heracles attacked the Amazon's capital city, Themyscira. Heracles subdued and ravaged the Amazon leader, Hippolyta, while his forces ransacked the city and enslaved the Amazons. When the Amazons finally fought their way to freedom, Hippolyta led her survivors to a remote island paradise that they named Themyscira in honor of their fallen city. On Paradise Island the Amazons began their new lives, erecting buildings and monuments, and perfecting their skills as artisans and warriors free from the often hostile and hateful influence of "man's world." In time, however, Hippolyta realized the value of reconciliation with the outside world. Commissioning Diana as Amazonian ambassador, Queen Hippolyta announces, "It is time again to open the lines of communication between man and woman—something I should have a done a long time ago."[4]

As ambassador of the Amazons, Diana preaches a message of peace and equality among men and women in an effort to restore the relationship between her people and the outside world. As ambassadors for Christ, Christians preach a similar message. According to Paul, God "gave us this wonderful message of reconciliation…. We speak for Christ when we plead, 'Come back to God!'" (2 Corinthians 5:19-20, NLT).

Just as the sins of Heracles and his men caused a rift between the Amazons and the outside world, our sins have caused a rift between God and humanity. The Bible says, "Your wrongs have separated you from your God" (Isaiah 59:2, GWT). Our message to the world is that God wants to restore the relationship broken by our sins, which he does through Jesus. This is why my family travels to comic book conventions all over the Midwest, giving away copies of *The Amazing Gospel*, a comic book adaptation of the story of Jesus. By sharing the message of Jesus—his life, death, and resurrection—we are being ambassadors for Christ. Of course, I don't always have a comic book gospel to hand someone, and, I'm guessing, neither do you. Thankfully, there are countless means by which to share God's message.

Few stories highlight Wonder Woman's role as ambassador as well as a single issue written by Phil Jimenez and Joe Kelly. In *Wonder Woman* #170, Lois Lane spends the day following Wonder Woman across the globe, experiencing for herself what a day in the life of the Amazon Princess is like.

In the morning, Wonder Woman speaks at a university in Marseilles, France, about Amazonian values, such as "trying to respect the basic rights of those around you and valuing each other simply because we exist." From there, Lois and Wonder Woman appear on a morning talk show, where Diana promotes the Wonder Woman Foundation. "I established the foundation," she explains, "to help me in my mission—spreading the precepts of the Amazons and my gods." The foundation teaches Amazonian methods of agriculture to farmers in ecologically damaged areas and builds schools in rural areas in the Americas and Africa where students learn respect and tolerance. Next, the duo travel to Washington DC, where Wonder Woman meets with the president to request funding for peacekeeping relief in multiple war zones. In Atlanta, Diana plays basketball with a group of boys whom she mentors. In Indonesia, she teaches self-defense to young women, mostly prostitutes. In Rwanda, she visits a refugee camp full of children, many of them dying of malnutrition and open wounds.[5]

Wonder Woman's activities mirror many Christian ministries across the globe, reminding us that actions often speak louder than words.

In a candid conversation with Steve Trevor, the fighter pilot who crashed on her island, Diana confesses, "As long as I can remember, I've had dreams of being the one who reunited Themyscira with the outside world; of being that bridge."[6] When we share the message of Christ, we get to be that bridge. Only we don't reunite a lost Amazon tribe with the outside world; rather, we reunite a lost world with a loving God.

OUR MOTIVATION

What motivates someone to become an ambassador? What's the driving force behind an ambassador's mission and message? What compels a potential ambassador to take action?

In William Marston's original telling of Wonder Woman's origins, the entire Amazon tribe was sculpted from clay by Aphrodite, the mythological goddess of love and beauty. In their creation, Aphrodite thinks to herself, "I shall breathe life into these women and also the power of love!" Thus, the Amazons are infused with the love of their creator.[7]

Fittingly, love becomes a motivating factor in Diana choosing to become the Amazon's emissary. When the American fighter pilot Steve Trevor crash lands on the island, Diana nurses him back to health, falling in love with him in the process. Her love for Steve motivates Diana to compete for the title of Wonder Woman despite her mother's protests.[8]

Love should likewise motivate Christians to be ambassadors for Christ. Paul puts it simply: "The love of Christ compels us" (2 Corinthians 5:14, NKJV). Just as the Amazons were infused with the love of their creator, Christians are infused with the love of Christ. The love of Jesus is the motivating force behind our mission. It's why we do what we do. It's why my family attends comic book conventions, hands out comics, visits cancer patients in children's hospitals, and does everything else related to our ministry.

When the love of God gets hold of you, it presses you into action. *The Message* version of the Bible renders Paul's words in this verse this way: "Christ's love has moved me to such extremes. His love has the first and last word in everything we do"(2 Corinthians 5:14, MSG).

Jesus loves us—personally, powerfully, passionately. On the cross he demonstrated how much he loves us. The Bible says, "God shows his love for us in that while we were still sinners, Christ died for us" (Romans 5:8, ESV). Jesus gave his life to win our heart. He stretched his arms out as wide as he could, as if to say, "I love you this much." And he had them nailed there, so we would never forget. And Jesus invites us to live in his love. He told his followers, "I have loved you even as the Father has loved me. Live within my love. When you obey me you are living in my love, just as I obey my Father and live in his love" (John 15:9-10, TLB).

Wonder Woman's mother once said something with a similar ring. In the last Wonder Woman story written by her creator, William Marston, Queen Hippolyta assures her daughter, "The only real happiness for anybody is to be found in obedience to loving authority."[9] Hippolyta's admonition resonates with an old hymn by Daniel Towner: "Trust and obey, for there's no other way to be happy in Jesus, than to trust and obey."

Jesus is our loving authority. As such, he invites us to live in his love and experience genuine joy by trusting him and obeying him. That's what happens when Christians rely on and live in the love of Jesus. His love makes us move. It compels us into action. His love has the first and last word in everything we do.

✻✻✻

Wonder Woman has embarked on countless adventures since her debut more than seventy years ago. She has tangled with opponents as diverse as the supervillain Cheetah, the intergalactic despot Darkseid, and even the mythological god Ares. But through it all she has remained true to her Amazonian assignment. She has a clear mission, a crucial message, and a compelling motivation. So do you. By being Christ-like, communicating God's message of reconciliation, and allowing the love of Christ to compel us, we fulfill our role as ambassadors of Christ.

NOTES

1. *Wonder Woman*, directed by Lauren Montgomery (Warner Home Video, 2009).

2. Mark Kelly, "Study: Unchurched Americans Turned Off by Church, Open to Christians," LifeWay Christian Resources, January 9, 2009, http://www.lifeway.com/Article/LifeWay-Research-finds-unchurched-Americans-turned-off-by-church-open-to-Christians.

3. William Messner-Loebs (writer) and Mike Deodato Jr. (artist), *Wonder Woman* #0 (DC Comics, 1994).

4. *Wonder Woman*, directed by Lauren Montgomery (Warner Home Video, 2009).

5. Phil Jimenez and Joe Kelly (writers), Andy Lanning (artist), "A Day in the Life," *Wonder Woman* #170 (DC Comics, 2001).

6. *Wonder Woman*, directed by Lauren Montgomery (Warner Home Video, 2009).

7. William Moulton Marston, *Wonder Woman* #1 (DC Comics, 1942).

8. William Moulton Marston, *All-Star Comics* #8 (DC Comics, 1941).

9. William Moulton Marston, *Wonder Woman* #23 (DC Comics, 1947).

18
THE FLASH

To this day, the coolest-looking superhero costume that I've ever seen onscreen is the one worn by John Wesley Shipp in CBS's 1990 television series *The Flash*. I was only nine years old when the series first aired, but I made sure never to miss an episode. *The Flash* was a remarkable and unforgettable series, which, of course, means that it was canceled after just one season! At least fans can now enjoy the CW's new Flash television series, starring Grant Gustin. In this new series John Wesley Shipp returns to play the Flash's father, Henry Allen.

I enjoyed the opportunity to meet John Wesley Shipp at a recent convention. When I asked him what he enjoys most about having played the Flash and now playing the Flash's father, he spoke of the "passing of the baton" and the many connections that he shares with Grant Gustin. When I shared a copy of *The Amazing Gospel* and one of our Costumers for Christ pamphlets with him, he immediately lit up. The son of a retired Baptist preacher, John eagerly spoke of his father's faith and the impact it had on his life and career. Afterward, John posed for pictures with me wearing my own Flash costume—a humble spandex bodysuit adorned by bright yellow accents. It may not look nearly as impressive as the one John Wesley Shipp wore, but I think it still does the Scarlet Speedster justice.

The Flash—as every comic fan knows—is the fastest man alive. In a freak accident, a bolt of lightning exploded through the window of police scientist Barry Allen's crime lab, striking a shelf full of chemicals. Doused in the electrified chemicals, Barry's body chemistry began to change, and he discovered that he could run, think, and react at super-speed. Barry then uses his newfound swiftness to stop criminals in their tracks as the Scarlet Speedster, aka the Flash.

Barry Allen isn't the original super-speedster though, and I'm not thinking about Jay Garrick.[1] Tucked away in the ancient book of 1 Kings is a little-known story about Elijah. As one of God's primary prophets in the Old Testament, Elijah performed more than a few miracles. But in this instance, the Bible says, "Then the LORD gave special strength to Elijah. He tucked his cloak into his belt and ran ahead of Ahab's chariot all the way to the entrance of Jezreel" (1 Kings 18:46, NLT). God granted Elijah "special strength" and enough super-speed to outrun a chariot across miles of desert! Apparently, not all superheroes are found in comic books.

While you may not have been struck by lightning or endowed by the Lord with miraculous speed, every Christian has a race to run. The Bible says this:

> Therefore, since we are surrounded by such a huge crowd of witnesses to the life of faith, let us strip off every weight that slows us down, especially the sin that so easily trips us up. And let us run with endurance the race God has set before us. We do this by keeping our eyes on Jesus, the champion who initiates and perfects our faith. (Hebrews 12:1-2, NLT)

We humans have a tendency to quit too soon, to stop before we cross the finish line. Our inability to finish what we start is evidenced in the smallest of things: a partly mowed lawn, a half-read book, a short-lived diet. We don't want to do the same thing with the race that God has set before us. This short passage offers three instructions for running the Christian race with endurance, reinforcing lessons that we can glean from the Flash.

FINDING YOUR ENCOURAGEMENT

In the comics, Barry Allen has a nephew named Wally West. At just ten years old, Wally adores the Flash, so Barry arranges a meeting between young Wally and his alter ego in the crime lab. But lightning strikes twice as the same electrified chemicals douse Wally and imbue him with the same super-speed that his uncle Barry has. Wally dons a brightly colored suit and becomes the Flash's sidekick, Kid Flash. Years later, in DC's epic crossover event *Crisis on Infinite Earths*, Barry sacrifices himself to prevent the universe from ripping apart. In honor of his mentor, Wally takes up the mantle of the Flash. His uncle Barry's heroism inspires Wally to keep running. In *Flash* #74, Wally recalls, "Barry Allen sacrificed his life to save the universe. In tribute, I took his name and identity…. He's the greatest hero I've ever known. And I'm proud to follow in his footsteps."[2]

Just as Wally was encouraged to run the race set before him by the legacy of his predecessor, Christians are encouraged to run the race set before us by the heroes of faith in whose steps we follow. Hebrews 12:1 refers to a "huge crowd of witness to the life of faith." Their names and deeds are listed in the preceding chapter, Hebrews 11. Some call it the Bible's Hall of Faith. I like to call it the Bible's Hall of Heroes.

These biblical heroes don't wear spandex or fly around in capes, but they instill us with hope, optimism, and faith. They were men and women who overthrew kingdoms, stood for justice, protected God's messengers, and faced down ferocious lions, unquenchable fires, and belligerent giants. They put whole armies to flight.

Their weaknesses were turned to strengths because of their faith in God.

Their stories encourage us. When you're struggling to understand why bad things happen to good people, read the story of Joseph. When you feel inadequate for the task at hand, read about Moses. When you're facing the giants of fear, failure, doubt, or discouragement, read the story of David and discover how he toppled his giant. In fact, just go read Hebrews 11 and see what God did in the lives of ordinary people such as Sarah, Gideon, Rahab, and Jephthah.

And it isn't just biblical heroes who encourage us; personal heroes of faith can inspire us just as much. Just as John Wesley Shipp's father set an example of faith for him, my mother set an example early in my life about the importance of faith, family, and following Jesus. I hope to set that same example for my children. Perhaps you have a mother, father, grandmother, Sunday school teacher, or some other person who influenced you to begin your Christian walk, and that person still encourages you to run with endurance. Their lives and those of biblical heroes prove that a life of faith is possible in spite of all sorts of adversity. And even now, from heaven's stadium, they cheer us on, encouraging us to follow in their footsteps.

FORSAKING YOUR ENTANGLEMENTS

Although they lack the wider recognition of the villains who pester Batman and Superman, the enemies of the Flash form a memorable rogues' gallery through their unique blend of colorful costumes, diverse powers, and unusual abilities. The Flash's collection of nemeses includes such inventive villains as the Mirror Master, Captain Cold, Weather Wizard, and Captain Boomerang. But, perhaps the most eclectic criminal in the Flash's rogues' gallery is the Trickster.

The Trickster always looks for new ways to trip up the Flash—literally. In the original television series, the Flash falls for one of the oldest tricks in the book when the Trickster, played by Mark Hamill, dumps a trunk load of marbles all over the city street. When Flash races around the corner, he trips and tumbles across the marbles, finally falling on his backside. "I'd laugh," he admits, "if not for the dead body in there."[3]

Christians may not face costume-clad villains with alliterated names, but we do face an obstacle that's continually tripping us up: sin. Again, Hebrews says, "Let us strip off every weight that slows us down, especially the sin that so easily trips us up" (Hebrews 12:1, NLT). Another translation calls it "the sin that so easily entangles" us (NIV).

That's what sin does. It slows us down, trips us up, and entangles us. What sin trips you up? Is it anger or maybe addiction? It could be pride or prejudice. Perhaps you're weighed down by lustful eyes or a lying tongue. Maybe it's selfishness or sexual promiscuity. For many of you reading this, it's a no-brainer to figure out what sin trips you up. We know which obstacles in our lives cause us to stumble and fall over and over again. These sins weigh us down and keep us from moving toward the finish line. That's why it's so important for us to watch our step and avoid the sins that trip us up.

Of course, sin isn't the only thing that holds us back. Hebrews also reminds us to strip off "every weight" that slows us down. These "weights" can include fear (as we saw with Green Lantern), or anger (as we saw with the Hulk), or negative influences and isolation (as we saw with Cyborg). Our "weights" can include an unhealthy relationship, a bad habit, or even an addiction to social media—anything that hinders us from running the race God has set before us. The Flash wears a sleek, skintight suit for a reason: aerodynamics. The less weight we carry, the faster we'll run and the stronger we'll finish.

FIXING YOUR EYES

In the pilot episode of the 1990s television series, Barry Allen first discovers his incredible speed when attempting to catch a city bus. Suddenly, Barry speeds right passed the bus, whipping his head around as he passes it. Not watching where he's going, Barry zooms down the street and out of the city, finally crashing into the waters of Crystal Beach thirty miles away. A trio of bystanders pulls Barry out of the water and onto the shore, his clothes tattered and torn from the impact. Confused and coughing up water, Barry mutters, "What happened?"[4]

Christians can experience a similar crash and splash if we allow ourselves to be distracted, which is why the Bible says, "And let us run with endurance the race God has set before us. We do this by keeping our eyes on Jesus, the champion who initiates and perfects our faith" (Hebrews 12:1-2, NLT). Fixing our eyes on Jesus enables us to avoid distractions, stay on course, and faithfully finish the race that God marked off for us.

When I was about seven or eight years old, my dad taught me a valuable lesson, even though he didn't realize it at the time. On a sweltering summer day in Louisiana, the humidity can make you feel like you're trekking through the Amazon rainforest. The fact that our front lawn looked a bit like a jungle didn't help matters. So, my father decided to teach me how to mow the lawn. My dad primed the little 1.5 horsepower engine and gave the starter a strong pull, and then he turned the roaring red monster over to me. The vibrations ran straight through my eight-year-old hands, up my arms and to my teeth, which chattered like a wind-up toy.

My dad sat back and watched as I cut a zigzag pattern from one end of the lawn to the other. That wavy pattern continued for several passes until, after giving up hopes that my aim would improve by itself, my dad finally stopped me. He told me not to look right in front of the mower and definitely not to look all around the yard; rather, he said, pick a spot on the opposite side of the yard and fix my eyes on the spot. It took some time and practice, but by focusing on where I wanted to be rather than where I was, I finally mowed a straight path through the yard.

Jesus does the same for us. He is the North Star of our faith. If you align your life with Jesus, fixing your eyes on him, then you can you can stay on the straight and narrow. I'll warn you, though: if you really commit your life to following Jesus, there may be people who don't understand your determination.

Barry knows what that's like. In one of his opening monologues from the current television series, Barry explains, "When I was a child, I saw my mother killed by something impossible. My father went to prison for her murder. Then an accident made me the impossible. To the outside world, I'm just an ordinary forensic scientist, but secretly I use my speed to fight crime and find others like me, and one day I'll find who killed my mother and get justice for my father."[5] Throughout most of the first season, Barry's adoptive family and fellow police officers don't understand his commitment to solving his mother's murder. They think that Barry simply imagined the yellow-clad speedster whom he claims killed his mom. But Barry stayed focused, and because he did, he finally crossed the finish line, confronting his mother's killer and clearing his father's name.

People may think that you're deluded for following Christ instead of following the crowd, but if you fix your eyes on Jesus, you'll cross your own finish line. The Bible urges us, "Don't you realize that in a race everyone runs, but only one person gets the prize? So run to win! All athletes are disciplined in their training. They do it to win a prize that will fade away, but we do it for an eternal prize" (1 Corinthians 9:24-25, NLT).

What is that prize? It's Jesus. Jesus set the course and plotted its path, and now he awaits us at the finish line. Our race ends in the arms of Christ. Not only will we spend eternal life *with* Jesus, but we'll finally be *like* Jesus. When our race is over, the Bible says, "we shall be like him, for we shall see him as he is" (1 John 3:2, NIV).

In the comics, the Flash can channel his inertia through the Speed Force, which allows him to share his speed with other objects or people in motion. In other words, Flash can temporarily make others like him. That's what Jesus promises to do for us—only it won't be temporary. He promises to share his life, his righteousness, and his glory with us forever. That's a prize worth running for, don't you think?

***

The Flash may be the fastest man alive, but in the Christian race speed doesn't matter. What matters is that we find encouragement in the examples of the heroes who've run ahead of us, that we break free of the sin that so easily entangles us, and that we fix our eyes on Jesus—the champion of our faith. In the end, it's not about how fast your run, but how faithfully you finish.

NOTES

1. Jay Garrick was DC Comics's original Flash. He first appeared in 1940, but was later replaced by Barry Allen in 1956, ushering in the Silver Age of comics.

2. Mark Waid (writer) and Greg LaRoque (artist), "Trust," *Flash* (2nd series) #74 (DC Comics, 1993).

3. "Tricksters," *The Flash: The Complete Series* #17 (Warner Home Video, 2010).

4. "Pilot," *The Flash: The Complete Series* #1 (Warner Home Video, 2010).

5. "The Man in the Yellow Suit," *The Flash* #9 (CW Network, 2014).

CONCLUSION

Who is your favorite superhero, and why? That's a question that kids and comic book fans alike pose on a regular basis. I recently posted this question on Facebook and received some insightful responses.

■ Brian replies, "Superman. His powers are beyond imagination, yet he uses them to solve problems that normal humans can't. Whether it's a global threat or a cat trapped in a tree, he places our welfare above his own."

■ Laura writes, "Huntress. Because she is an anti-hero who struggles between right and wrong. I think that's very human and relatable."

■ Mark explains, "Growing up, my favorite superhero was always Spider-Man because he was an ordinary guy just trying to do the right thing. 'With great power comes great responsibility' is a powerful ideal to live by."

■ Mike comments, "I always wanted to have Magneto's powers. Even today I still try to move objects across the room with the wave of my hand…. I fail every time."

■ Kelly responds, "Black Canary, because she's a survivor. She's been through some of the worst things that a hero could endure and still retains her faith in humanity. She sees the best in people and strives to offer redemption to those who seem like they could be brought back to the right path."

■ Zac says, "Superman. He's virtually all-powerful, yet incorruptible. He is completely kind and loving despite the fact that he could enslave or destroy us in an afternoon if he chose to."

■ Steve says, "Batman is my favorite. I love his backstory and how he basically gives his life (mentally, physically, and financially) to help Gotham."

■ Jennifer replies, "Easy! Wonder Woman. The lasso of truth! The invisible jet! Plus, since I'm only four feet tall, I always wanted to be an Amazon princess."

■ Rusty answers, "The Blue Beetle. He has the intelligence of Batman. The moral fortitude of Superman. The humor of Spider-Man. Plus, how can you not love a hero who likes to smile?"

■ Kristina says, "Aquaman was actually my first favorite because I love the water. His powers of being able to breathe underwater and communicate with aquatic life forms are ones I've always wished I had."

■ Mandy comments, "Iron Man I think is one of my faves because Tony Stark is a genius who acts the way I wish I could: confident and cleverly snarky."

■ Geoffrey replies, "Captain America. Technically, he has no superpowers, but when the war charge is led, he's always in the front of the pack. He's not as strong as the Hulk, not as God-like as Thor, not as rich as Tony Stark, but these guys would follow him to the ends of the earth if need be."

■ Jeff's response may have been most fitting: "Superman, because of his likeness to Jesus."

Each of the heroes mentioned above and the others surveyed throughout this book embody a variety of virtues from courage to compassion, from perseverance to power, and from humility to honor. More importantly, each of them illustrates some biblical principle, reinforcing the timeless truths of God's Word and helping us draw nearer to the heart of God. Like the parables sprinkled throughout Jesus' preaching, the stories of heroic icons such as

Superman, Wonder Woman, Batman, Black Widow, and Spider-Man help comic book geeks like me connect with the teachings of God's Word in relevant and relatable ways. The only drawback is, these heroes aren't real.

Fictional heroes can be exciting, encouraging, and even educational. But at the end of the day, people need a real hero—a hero who catches us when we fall, who rescues us from evil, and who saves us not just for a time, but for eternity. We need a Holy Hero. This is why, whenever I'm asked about my favorite superhero, I tell people, "It's Jesus."

Last October I convinced nearly two dozen members of Blooming Grove Christian Church, our home congregation, to suit up as superheroes of all sorts for a local Halloween Parade. Together we built a Hall of Justice backdrop for a superhero-themed Last Supper. Jesus sat in the middle of the table surrounded by the likes of Cyclops, Wolverine, Invisible Girl, Thor, Batman, Superman, and many more. Splashed across the tablecloth in bold comic book font, we proudly proclaimed "Jesus is our Superhero" to hundreds of spectators! This is the message that I seek to share not just with the comic and cosplay subculture, but with all people.

Like Superman, Jesus is the only Son of his Father, sent from above to save the world. He personifies the truth and justice that Lois Lane pursues. He offers second chances just like Nick Fury did for Black Widow. Like Batman, he seeks to build a worldwide family of followers. Similar to the Green Lantern Corps, Jesus is fearless and urges us to fear less. Jesus reveals the true scope and significance of love, calling us to harness the power and serve the cause of love like the Star Sapphires. He channels sanctified anger toward righteous ends even better than the Hulk. He wields greater power with greater responsibility than Spider-Man. Like the X-Men, Jesus suffered persecution from the very people he came to save, yet he loved his enemies and prayed for the soldiers who pierced him.

Most importantly, like the Flash, Jesus gave his life to save you and me. That's the definition of a hero.

So the next time someone asks you, "Who's your favorite super-hero?" I hope you'll join me in proudly proclaiming, "Jesus is the greatest superhero of them all!"

The Gospel According to Dr. Seuss
Snitches, Sneetches, and Other Creachas
James W. Kemp

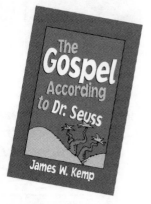

JUDSON PRESS
PUBLISHERS SINCE 1824